SPECIAL NEEDS IN ORDINARY SCHOOLS
General editor: Peter Mittler
Associate editors: Mel Ainscow, Brahm Norwich, Peter Pumfrey and
Sheila Wolfendale

2 2 JUN 2022

WITHDRAWN

Inclusive Mathematics 5–11

Also available from Continuum:

Peter Benton and Tim O'Brien: *Special Needs and the Beginning Teacher*
Asher Cashdan and Lyn Overall: *Teaching in Primary Schools*
Paul Croll and Diana Moses: *Special Needs in the Primary School*
Julie Dockrell and David Messer: *Children's Language and
    Communication Difficulties*
Alan Dyson *et al.*: *New Directions in Special Needs*
Anthony Orton: *Pattern in the Teaching and Learning of Mathematics*
Anthony Orton: *Learning Mathematics*

Inclusive Mathematics 5–11

Brian Robbins

CONTINUUM
London and New York

Continuum
Wellington House   370 Lexington Avenue
125 Strand   New York
London WC2R 0BB   NY 10017–6503

First published 2000

British Library Cataloguing-in-Publication Data
A catalogue record for this book is available from the British Library.

ISBN 0–8264–4792–9

Typeset by BookEns Ltd, Royston, Herts
Printed and bound in Great Britain by Martins the Printers Ltd,
Berwick upon Tweed

Contents

Foreword

Peter Mittler

The revised National Curriculum, launched in September 2000, reflects the strongest and clearest commitment to the principles and practice of inclusion so far from any government of this country. Equality of opportunity is at the core of a statement of values underpinning the whole curriculum. Each document includes a 7-page statement on inclusion, with guidance on setting suitable learning challenges, responding to pupils' diverse needs and overcoming potential barriers to learning and assessment for individuals and groups of pupils. These principles are developed for each subject area of the curriculum.

This is all very different from the 1988 curriculum, when children with special educational needs were first overlooked and then added as an afterthought. A great deal of work has been done by teachers on the ground in making the curriculum accessible to all pupils and, in working with official bodies such as the Qualifications and Curriculum Authority, to develop guidelines on access and entitlement. Inclusion depends on children experiencing success in learning and that in turn depends on a curriculum which is designed to be accessible to all. It also depends on the development of a range of supports tailored to the distinctive needs of individuals and groups at a particular time.

This book could hardly be more timely. Its publication coincides not only with the new curriculum but with the full implementation of the National Numeracy Strategy in all schools. The additional guidance provided here is based on a wealth of experience of mainstream and special schools and will be all the more welcome because mathematics has received so much less attention than literacy.

University of Manchester
March 2000

Acknowledgements

I would like to thank all those teachers and children, too many to mention, who have shown me what mathematics can be when it is approached with imagination and enthusiasm.

I would also wish to recognize the influence of two great educators, Ron Gulliford who taught me to ask 'why' and Tim Brighouse who helped me to see that the impossible is just the inevitable waiting to happen.

Thanks are also due to Anthony Haynes and Alan Worth at Continuum, to Elizabeth Leroy, who copy-edited the text, and to Frank Merrett, who compiled the Index.

And a special debt of gratitude to my wife Fran for her encouragement and for taking over my duties on our small farm when deadlines approached.

Introduction

'You have the freedom to be yourself, your true self, here and now, and nothing can stand in your way.'

from *Jonathan Livingston Seagull*,
who challenged expectations (Bach, 1972)

LOW ACHIEVEMENT IN MATHEMATICS

Is it inevitable that children with special educational needs will be less successful in mathematics than their peers? Teachers know that pupils in special education have difficulty in meeting national standards and research evidence supports this view (O'Toole and O'Toole, 1989). As a consequence of their pupils' low achievement there has been an assumption that mainstream developments in mathematics teaching are not appropriate for special education.

This book challenges the notion that children with special educational needs (SEN) should be excluded from the mathematics curriculum experienced by other children. It brings together two current strands of educational development, (a) inclusion and (b) raising achievement in mathematics, and promotes the principle that the mathematics curriculum in primary schools should encompass the needs and learning characteristics of all children.

To succeed, inclusive mathematics must operate in three contexts: the classroom, the school and in the opportunities teachers have for continued professional development. It is therefore written bearing in mind teachers; headteachers; mathematics coordinators and special educational needs coordinators (SENCOs) in primary and special schools; advisory and support teachers; and tutors of mathematics courses and of special education courses. It is designed to be a useful source book for students undergoing initial training and for teachers on professional development courses.

AN INTERNATIONAL PERSPECTIVE

The growth of a global economy brings with it a global view. Comparisons are made between the relative economic success of countries as, increasingly, educational standards are seen as a key element in competitiveness. Prime Minister Tony Blair proclaimed in his election campaign that the priorities of his government would be 'education, education and education'. The subsequent thrust of action related to schools has been towards the raising of standards for all children, including those with special educational needs.

The debate on standards has become an ever-present part of the educational and political scene in many countries. They are seen as falling or rising and various people are credited with praise or blame. Teachers have had to bear the brunt of this criticism, much of which centres on literacy and mathematics. Both are the subject of government initiatives in Britain.

In Chapter 3 we will consider recent developments in mathematics teaching in primary education in several countries. We will draw upon the experiences of teachers in Hungary, Ireland, The Netherlands and the United Kingdom.

LITERACY AND NUMERACY

The daily Literacy Hour is established in England and Wales and teachers are adapting to what many feel is the most significant challenge to their methodology since the introduction of the National Curriculum. This is being quickly followed by the Numeracy Strategy which demands that at least 45 minutes each day are devoted to a lesson that follows the Framework for Numeracy (DfEE, 1999). The implementation of the Numeracy Strategy is addressed in the second part of this book.

'Differentiation' was mentioned in the National Curriculum orders and this has been taken as being the means of solving the problems that prevented children with SEN from participating in the National Curriculum (Daniels and Anghileri, 1995) but teachers have been frustrated at the lack of guidance as to what exactly was intended by this phrase. Guidance on teaching pupils with severe learning difficulties was forthcoming (NCC, 1992), but by then the feeling had firmly taken root that children with special needs were an afterthought. There were mixed messages coming from special schools, where some teachers were sceptical about the value of teaching the National Curriculum to children who faced significant difficulties in all areas of life and for whom an academic education was seen as totally inappropriate. Other teachers in special schools wholeheartedly embraced the principle that all children were entitled to receive the National Curriculum and saw it as their role to make it suitable (Ashdown *et al.*, 1991). Certainly, in terms of mathematics, Williams (1992) reports that both special and mainstream schools expressed the intention of keeping to a minimum the disapplication of pupils from the National Curriculum.

The recommendation of the Dearing Committee (SCAA, 1994) that the Curriculum should be wholly meaningful and relevant went some way to meeting the objections and gave scope for the needs of individual pupils to be taken into account when planning the school curriculum.

STANDARDS

Projects and initiatives aimed at raising standards, such as the National Curriculum in the UK, have not always been planned with due regard to the needs of children with SEN. There appears to have been an assumption that initiatives to raise standards will have an impact across the whole school population. It is only later the realization dawns that there are some pupils who will confound this notion.

Concern about standards leads, quite rightly, to a search for ways of raising achievement and it is common to look to other countries that are considered to be doing better. Japan is seen as having higher standards of achievement, although there is debate about whether the price of mental disturbance among Japanese schoolchildren is a price worth paying. The pressure under which children find themselves in Japan is one of the cultural differences that have to be taken into account before these comparisons can be considered valid (Burkhardt, 1999; Hoyles *et al.*, 1999).

Hungary, which is considered to produce the best mathematicians, has proved to be a more popular model and is being influential in the UK's Numeracy Strategy.

An obvious solution to the standards issue is to bring everyone up to an acceptable level. This has been defined in many countries as a series of predetermined norms that children are expected to have achieved by a specified age. Some will achieve a higher level, others will fall below. The British government's aim is that, by 2002, 75 per cent of 11-year-olds will have reached an age-appropriate standard in mathematics. Chapter 3 will include some of the criteria used to measure whether a child has reached the expected level.

THE EXCLUDED 20 PER CENT?

The percentages stated above carry the assumption that over 20 per cent of children will not reach that level. Is it a coincidence that one in five is, according to the Warnock Report (DES, 1978), the proportion of children with special educational needs? The logic of setting a 75 per cent target would appear to be that it is unrealistic to expect children with special educational needs to achieve as much as children without SEN. When we look at impediments to learning in Chapter 2 we will see that there are seemingly overwhelming difficulties in raising the attainment of the lowest achievers to the level of the average in mainstream education. On the other hand we must challenge the unfairness of setting a predetermined failure rate that will legitimize low expectations of some pupils.

WORDS THAT CLARIFY AND CONFUSE

In any such discussion a number of terms creep in, such as achievement, attainment, levels, grades, norms and standards, which are often used synonymously. Each has a specific meaning but the distinctions become blurred when these terms become part of a public debate.

Achievement is taken to mean the whole range of personal success, much broader than academic successes.

Attainment is success measured by specified norms, which are usually performance criteria, such as 'can add whole numbers within the range 1 to 10'.

A set of such norms would be taken as indicating that a child had reached one of a series of sequential Levels of Attainment. In the UK the National Curriculum is built around ten levels, and Standard Assessment Tasks taken by pupils at 7, 11 and 14 years of age place them on a particular level in each of the core subjects; English (or Welsh if that is their language of instruction), mathematics and science.

Grades can mean either marks that you receive for a piece of work or, in some countries, such as the USA, refers to the sequential organization of teaching groups. In the UK this is designated by 'Years' from Year R (Reception), referring to children in the first year of compulsory education who will have reached 5 years of age by 31 August. Year 1 children will have reached 6 years of age by that date and Year 2 will have reached 7. Each age group is then identified by a year number up to 16-year-olds (Year 11).

Standards is a word that has lost its currency due to overuse. In current usage it refers to a measure against which judgements can be made about achievement in different countries and at different times in history. The popular media has become adept at selecting research evidence to support their particular story line. At the time when the British press was running a campaign against teachers and so-called 'modern methods', a typical story was that reading standards were falling. One newspaper justified a banner headline to that effect with the evidence that 'forty-eight per cent of primary school children were below average in reading' [*sic*]. What hope had teachers got when statistics can be employed with such devastating simplicity! Many of the stories that set out to demonstrate the relatively poor position of a country in league tables of academic performance show a similar lack of logical rigour.

INCLUSION OF CHILDREN WITH SEN

Another global move is the one towards the inclusion of children with special educational needs within the mainstream of education. This is often portrayed as children with a wide diversity and degree of individual learning difficulties being educated together in the same class. This creates an additional challenge for the teacher and it is the commitment of the teacher and the support available in the school that will determine whether children with SEN are successfully included in the class. Chapter 6 will draw upon teaching observed in primary classrooms in several countries.

A 100 per cent target for both inclusion and the achievement of age-appropriate standards in mathematics is the logical long-term goal to both movements. This would carry the unfortunate possibility of having to exclude certain pupils from the norms because of the severity of their learning difficulties, a tactic used to maintain schools' positions in achievement league tables. This would be in conflict with the principles of inclusion.

The title of this book sets a challenge to all concerned in primary education to include many more pupils in these targets and in the measures being followed to achieve them. It is not about setting targets that are currently unrealistic but about recognizing that advances are constantly being made in overcoming the impediments to learning faced by some children. It is about promoting a process of development in teaching methods that will reduce that 20 per cent to 10 per cent, then 5 per cent, then 1 per cent, then . . .? In short, it is about children, in Brighouse's phrase, doing 'better than their previous best'. He believes that we are on the verge of 'a great leap forward in whole-school and pupil success' (Brighouse and Woods, 1999). Within such an advance should be the means to improve the mathematical achievement of our lowest-attaining pupils. That would have a significant impact on overall educational standards and would be a vindication for inclusive approaches.

The title of this author's first published work, *Step by Small Step* (Robbins, 1978) borrows the words Neil Armstrong used when he became the first man to step onto the moon's surface; 'One small step for man, one giant leap for mankind.' The book resulted from an endeavour to include pupils, who had previously been considered ineducable, in the mathematics curriculum of a special school. If we set their achievements against those of the majority of children in mainstream schools then the phrase 'small step' was indeed nearer to the mark than 'giant leap'. None the less progress was made, through this and similar work, in developing a curriculum appropriate for pupils with severe learning difficulties (Ashdown *et al.*, 1991).

Terms such as 'entitlement' and 'access' are intended to remove the partition between those who will achieve and those who will not. There is concern that the term 'special educational needs' is inappropriate within an inclusive approach. In the absence of a term which has as wide a currency, 'SEN' has been used so far in this text to identify pupils who are thus described by the school system in which they are educated. This varies from country to country and may in some cases be confined only to those attending special schools, whilst in other countries it may refer to a much larger section of the school population (Meijer, 1998).

It is clear, then, that the term SEN is a very general one and has limited value. For the purpose of this book we need to establish a terminology that is related more specifically to the kind of differentiation that is needed by individual pupils.

The term 'low attainers' has been used to refer to those who are educated in mainstream schools but have not achieved the age-appropriate norms (Denvir *et al.*, 1982). They are not necessarily the same pupils as those identified as SEN but there is likely to be a considerable overlap and whether or not they are so labelled is unimportant, as our concern is with raising achievement.

We will use *low attainer* to refer to those who are part of a mainstream class but find it difficult, for whatever reason, to maintain the pace of the majority of the class. Teachers will attempt to give particular attention to these pupils within lessons and might arrange additional sessions to go over some of the work they find difficult. This will be considered under the term *additional support.*

This leaves us with the problem of identifying in shorthand terms those for whom traditionally an alternative to being in a mainstream class would have been considered preferable. For the sake of this text we will move to adopt a descriptor based on the degree of support that would be appropriate for particular pupils and use the term *regular individual support.* This will be taken to refer to those who need extra support, modifications to tasks or some other kind of differentiation in order to be able to participate in the topic being followed by the whole class.

These terms are arbitrary in that they depend to some extent on the perceptions of particular teachers and are not fixed by measures of intelligence or scores in assessment tests. Two different teachers might have differing views on which descriptor was appropriate for an individual pupil. There is also the danger that by adopting two descriptors, additional support and regular individual support, we are reverting to labelling. Whilst recognizing that possibility, the merit of using these terms is that, without some kind of commonly understood descriptor, the text could become turgid and repetitive.

CHANGING PERCEPTIONS

We must recognize that the level of individual support is not fixed but can vary according to the activity, to the skill of the teacher, to the growing self-confidence of the pupil, to the attitudes of the rest of the class and to a number of other variables. This book will set out to influence those variables by establishing a working model for including all pupils in the mathematics curriculum. It will build on four cornerstones.

The first one is that mathematics is a living medium through which ideas, facts and hypotheses are communicated. Too often it is seen as a dry and forbidding subject that demands a particular type of intelligence to master. The popular view is that many fail and few succeed. That impression is overturned when you observe a lively lesson led by an imaginative teacher. You realize that the memories of maths lessons those pupils will take into adulthood will be very different from the daunting stereotype that exists amongst the present generation.

The second is that *differentiation* is an essential skill for teachers. Rather than attempt a definition of differentiation, which can mean many things to many people, it will be explored through examples of practice in Part Two and the implications will be considered in Part Three.

Thirdly, inclusion is the accepted way forward for education. The Salamanca statement (UNESCO, 1994), signed in 1994 by representatives of 92 governments and 25 international organizations, has signalled a worldwide trend towards inclusive education and has ensured that inclusion remains very firmly on the agenda for everyone involved in special education.

Finally, school improvement is a powerful means of establishing inclusive practices. We are being encouraged to move away from terminology such as 'integration' which involves making special arrangements to enable pupils with 'special needs' to gain access to the education on offer. Instead we are encouraged to envisage special needs as an integral part of the provision made for all the pupils in a school (Ainscow, 1997).

INCLUSIVE MATHEMATICS

The term 'inclusive mathematics' embodies a set of principles that create the conditions for the growth within a school of a mathematics curriculum that encompasses the needs, expectations and aspirations of all pupils, that motivates them and enriches their school experience.

Those principles are that all pupils in primary education, without exception, will:

- experience a broad and rich mathematical education
- be expected to do better than their perceived best
- participate in projects and initiatives aimed at improving the teaching and learning of mathematics
- benefit from a flexible approach
- have their achievements celebrated
- benefit from their teachers having the confidence to identify their own strengths and weaknesses in teaching mathematics
- experience a dynamic, not restricted, approach to teaching
- experience mathematics as an international language and use it as an effective means of communication with people beyond the school
- benefit from an active commitment, within the school and beyond, that everyone is entitled to enjoy success in mathematics.

In Chapter 5 we will identify some of the practical implications of implementing these principles and in Chapter 13 we will consider ways of establishing the progress that a school is making towards achieving these principles.

The theme throughout the book will be that the learning needs of individual children can be met through a mainstream curriculum; the second part of the book has examples of current practice drawn from several countries. In each case the school is moving beyond the stage of providing alternative, watered-down activities for those pupils who do not meet the norms of the age group. None would claim to have arrived at the ideal contained in the statement of principles but all are working on the premiss that if primary mathematics teaching is to be inclusive it must be so from the planning stage, not be adapted at the point of delivery.

It will promote the principle that pupils with very different special needs can participate in the mathematics curriculum. Case studies will be used to illustrate a wide range of approaches where teachers have included pupils with particular types of learning needs in mathematics lessons.

MAKING MATHEMATICS TEACHING MORE INCLUSIVE

The approach in this book will not be to set out a 'counsel of perfection' nor, alternatively, to concede that children with special educational needs can only be taught effectively outside the mainstream curriculum.

It will promote the idea that primary schools can make considerable advances in making their mathematics teaching more inclusive than it has traditionally been and it will draw on existing good practice to support this assertion. According to the Centre for Studies on Inclusive Education there are four key factors in the development of an inclusive school: positive attitudes, suitable teaching styles and student groupings, adequate resources and effective parental involvement (CSIE 1996). Each of these will be addressed in this book.

At the end of each chapter will be one or two Talking Points that are intended as prompts for staff discussion.

Part One
Mathematics in primary and special schools

The importance of mathematics

Mathematics serves three roles; servant, citizen and sovereign.
(Higginson, 1999)

MATHEMATICS: A UNIVERSAL SUBJECT

Mathematics as a subject is present in the curriculum taught in most parts of the world and in the UK it is one of the three core subjects of the National Curriculum, together with English and science (DES, 1988). The Application of Number is also one of core skills in the National Vocational Qualifications (RSA, 1997), together with Communication Skills, Information and Communication Technology, Personal Skills and Problem-Solving Skills.

In Higginson's first sense, mathematics as the servant, it is a set of useful tools that should be available to everyone. Secondly, as citizen, it is one of many disciplines that can contribute to the understanding of the world and of the various subjects through which children learn about their community, both local and global. The third sense, as sovereign, is of mathematics as a field worthy of study for its own sake.

The latter is the most difficult to conceive of as being relevant to children with special educational needs but we should not discount the possibility that some might find enjoyment in exploring mathematical ideas and phenomena.

LITERATE AND NUMERATE

To be literate and numerate is essential in a civilized society but of the two the ability to communicate with the written and spoken word is generally considered the more important. Illiteracy is regarded as unacceptable, whereas many people will proclaim with a degree of pride that they are 'no good at maths'. It would certainly be quite surprising to see the majority of passengers on an aeroplane solving mathematical puzzles rather than reading books. Yet without mathematics aeroplanes would not fly, books would not be published and civilization itself would not have happened. At the more mundane, personal, level an individual who did not possess certain basic mathematical skills would face many difficulties in the daily routine of life.

REASONS FOR LEARNING MATHEMATICS

Denvir (Denvir *et al.*, 1982) puts forward the following reasons for learning mathematics:

- to acquire the basic skills for everyday life
- to develop the ability to think logically
- to encourage an independent approach to learning by equipping children with the skills of observation, recording and appraisal of information
- to provide a wide range of interesting experiences
- to use mathematics as a means of understanding the environment
- to gain skills that will be needed in adult life
- to develop each pupil's full potential.

Hoyles and her fellow writers (1999) consider that 'mathematics has roles beyond the basic functionality associated with numeracy and algebra'. They see it as 'a powerful language for sharing and systematizing knowledge, and as a part of human culture'. There is certainly a danger in reducing mathematics to the merely functional for low-attaining pupils, which in effect denies them the richness of mathematical experience available to their peers.

Brown (1999) regards this as a phenomenon peculiar to Western societies and points to central and eastern Europe and to the countries of the Pacific Rim where they give a greater emphasis to mathematics and aim to educate all children to the highest possible level.

The skills of everyday life

This can be demonstrated by tracking your daily routine. Getting up at the right time, filling the kettle, paying bills, filling the car with fuel, shopping, checking your bank statement, finding the channel you want on the television and using the telephone all require the application of some aspect of mathematics.

Bell (1992) believes that, when learning mathematics, children need to see it used in day-to-day situations. He sets out a set of activities that provide primary-aged children with opportunities to extend their use of mathematics beyond the maths lesson. For each topic — Shopping, Maths in the town, Houses and homes, Journeys, Sport, Time, Christmas and food — he gives suggestions for activities and classroom displays, as well as an indication of the links that occur with other curriculum areas.

Logical thought

The link between logic and mathematics was explored by Piaget, and his work has been influential in the past forty years (Piaget, 1952). From the young child trying to make sense of the world to the astronomer trying to make sense of the universe is admittedly a large step and the route has many pitfalls. Donaldson (1978) asks what happens during childhood to transform the enthusiastic young child into the bored adolescent. To take it a step further, does that interest become rekindled when in adulthood certain skills are found to be essential to running a home and keeping a job? Or has mathematics become such an unpleasant experience that some people avoid it whenever possible?

The reference earlier to the mathematics of everyday life might well have prompted a response along the lines 'that's obvious, but it's not the kind of mathematics that I mean.' The Assessment of Performance Unit (Joffe and Foxman, 1989) found that pupils do not associate 'everyday' problem-solving topics with mathematics. They, together with many other people, would regard the skills applied in daily life as being something quite different from the advanced application of mathematics practised in sixth forms, universities and specialized occupations. Indeed, it may not seem appropriate in a book on primary education to mention these higher-order skills, but it is this distinction that is one of the fundamental reasons for the discomfort that is felt by many people, including primary teachers.

Rhydderch-Evans (1989), who believes she suffered from 'maths phobia', refers to the feelings of failure engendered by the demands of correctness and regards this as another reason why so many people grow up with a negative view of the subject. This can have a detrimental affect on teaching, particularly in primary schools, where the teacher will be responsible for delivering most if not all of the curriculum. If teachers are comfortable with mathematics they can create an air of confidence in the classroom. If, however, they themselves feel uncertain about mathematics they are going to find it harder to set a positive example to the pupils.

A range of interesting experiences

The phrase 'interesting experiences' was commonly heard in staff-rooms and exemplified an approach that aimed to involve pupils in learning through their own activity. It was not unusual to see groups of pupils on High Streets taking a count of the traffic or recording the different types of shop. Price surveys, car registrations and bus numbers have all figured in this kind of activity. Rhydderch-Evans (1989) described how she set out to make mathematics a lively experience for her infant pupils. Certainly, the approaches involving observation, recording and appraisal of information promoted in publications such as the guidelines from Manchester College of Education (1971) seem far removed from the chanting of multiplication tables.

Pyke (1996) claims that efforts to make mathematics interesting have not resulted in sufficiently high standards. None the less, an interesting and motivating presentation of work is seen by Denvir (Denvir *et al.*, 1982) as a prerequisite for the successful teaching of low-attaining pupils.

Understanding the environment

Projects such as those suggested by Bell (1992) have the potential to give the children a far better understanding of their environment. One involves 6- and 7-year-olds in describing the journey they take to school. This is one of the key activities undertaken by mobility officers in helping children with visual handicaps to travel independently. When activities that in special schools have come under the heading of self-help and independence are analysed in terms of the skills involved they can legitimately be linked to the mathematics curriculum.

Independent learning

Another reason for the status of mathematics as a core subject is the need for these skills in other aspects of the curriculum. Achievement in science, technology and geography depend upon the ability to apply mathematical skills.

In science pupils need to know how to measure quantities, they need to be able to understand and use formulae and they need to be able to calculate. In geography they need to measure and calculate scale. Dimensions and scale also come into design and technology and in food preparation children will need to use weight, time and volume.

Foundation skills

The Cockroft Report (DES, 1982) demonstrates how mathematics provides the tool skills to perform a wide range of everyday activities. It includes a list of topics that the committee considered to be within the capability of most pupils. The foundation list of topics is set out under the following headings: number, percentages, use of calculator, money, time, measurement, graphs and pictorial representation, spatial concepts, ratio and proportion, statistical ideas.

Every child's potential

The process of translating this statement of intent in a school policy document into a living commitment that applies to every child is the purpose of this book. The extent of their potential achievement is an unknown and it is important that no ceiling is placed on the expectations of any pupil. The literature on disability has too many examples of children confounding the belief that they had limited capabilities for us to be that presumptuous. Against that we have to balance the heartache that could be caused by raising parents' hopes above a realistic level.

Numeracy

The Cockroft committee (DES, 1982) would expect a numerate person 'to appreciate and understand some of the ways in which mathematics can be used as a means of communication'. Numeracy is defined in the UK's National Numeracy Strategy as 'a proficiency which involves confidence and competence with numbers and measures' (DfEE, 1999). It goes on to state that numerate pupils would have the confidence to tackle problems on their own without seeking help and sets out some criteria for numeracy. These include an understanding of the number system, knowing by heart number bonds and multiplication tables and being able to use that knowledge to solve problems mentally, being able to calculate accurately and being able to interpret graphs, diagrams, charts and tables.

AIMS OF TEACHING MATHEMATICS

School policies on mathematics teaching will usually contain a set of aims and objectives, or goals. Denvir (Denvir *et al.*, 1982) categorizes them under three headings:

Useful: as a tool for the individual and society, e.g. social competence, vocational skills.
Cultural: as a part of our culture of which all pupils should have knowledge and experience.
Pleasurable: as a potential source of enjoyment.

The utilitarian reason is the one most usually stated when discussing the curricular needs of children who have learning difficulties. The rationale is that it is more important to concentrate on number recognition and computation and not to confuse them with aspects of the subject that are seen as irrelevant to their needs as adults.

This limited level of expectation is justified on the grounds that the effect of the complexity and severity of their disabling conditions make the task of teaching them the language and mathematics skills that most young children 'effortlessly acquire by the age of five or six years' [*sic*]. Whether nursery school staff would describe their job as effortless is another matter but it does draw attention to the gap in academic performance that has already developed during the early years of schooling. The average 5-, 6- and 7-year-old has already grasped mathematical ideas that people with severely disabling conditions may never possess.

In Part Two we will look at this in more detail and see how participation in a national mainstream project caused a similar school to rethink its teaching strategies. For the moment we will bear in mind that the statement in the Warnock Report (DES, 1978), that 'the aims of education are the same for all children', may be acceptable at a general level but might not stand up to the scrutiny of actual practice in special education. This begs the question as to whether it is realistic to expect all children to be able to thrive within a common set of aims or whether it is fairer to restate those aims at a functional level for those with significant learning difficulties. The driving force for containing the curriculum for all pupils within one general set of aims is the desire for those pupils to be included. The danger is that the curriculum is modified to such an extent that it appears unfamiliar to colleagues in mainstream schools.

The dilemma can be summarized as: do we expect all children to follow a common curriculum, at which some will probably fail, or do we limit the aims and adopt our teaching approach to the extent that some children experience a curriculum which is called 'mathematics' but consists of fragments of the mainstream mathematics curriculum?

This reflects the problem for mainstream education of, in Anderson's (1999) words, whether to 'cater for the needs of the minority who will eventually become professional mathematicians and at the same time equip the generally educated citizen and taxpayer with both the mathematical skills they will need and an appreciation of the role, place and power of mathematics as a discipline in its own right.'

It may be fanciful to think that children who face significant learning difficulties will ever aspire to be professional mathematicians, but they may find themselves in an occupation that demands something more than the ability to count and calculate. Educational communities resolve this issue in different ways. Some countries have separate schools at secondary level to cater for what are expressed as different life expectations (such as 'professional', 'technical' and 'vocational'), but in fact the placement of children is generally according to measures of ability. Others have a system of comprehensive education that purports to cater under one roof for children of all abilities.

In primary mathematics children will find themselves in classes with a much wider range of ability. Should the teacher expect the same of all children, even if that means putting some children through unmanageable hoops, in a spurious attempt to prove that they are no different from their normally developing peers?

The sensitivities that surround this issue are evident whenever one tries to find a term that distinguishes what have been called the 'handicapped' and the 'non-handicapped'. There is no doubt a difference at the extremes but it is less noticeable at the margins and the Warnock notion of a 'continuum of need' is helpful in trying to appreciate the qualitative distinction between special educational needs and low attainment. This distinction is not easily made and the close relationship of the criteria for each suggest it may not be fruitful to attempt it. Perhaps it would be more sensible to take the cue from the Warnock Committee and consider a 'continuum of aims'.

The present author was amongst those who argued for including children with SEN in the National Curriculum (Robbins, 1989) and this reflected a common desire not to be 'left out'. Halpin and Lewis (1996) later surveyed 12 English special schools on the appropriateness of the National Curriculum for their pupils. They found a range of responses, from anxiety about implementing the National Curriculum to the letter to a more relaxed approach. The latter was epitomized by a head teacher who said that his school had developed what they saw as appropriate curricula and then related them to the National Curriculum.

Another kind of modification that has been seen in both special and mainstream schools is the 'reduced curriculum', which will be covered in more detail in Chapter 4. In its extreme manifestation the 'irrelevant' and the difficult have been cut out and the pupils' mathematical diet is limited to practising computation and recording. This results in them being given additional practice work, often in the form of worksheets, when the rest of the class is exploring other mathematical ideas.

It is unfortunate that this line of thinking precludes such pupils from a rich source of enjoyment that might encourage a more positive view of the subject. This need not be so and reference will be made later in this book to activities that have involved pupils of all levels of ability.

NEEDS, EXPECTATIONS AND ASPIRATIONS

At the level of individual children with SEN, the focus of curriculum planning is usually on their identified needs, as defined in the multidisciplinary assessment that resulted in special provision being made for them. The emphasis is on finding out what is wrong and remedying it or alleviating a severely disabling condition.

There is a growing recognition that adolescent young people with SEN have a right to express their views on the kind of provision that would be appropriate for them when they leave school. With a set curriculum in primary education this kind of self-advocacy is not normally allowed for with younger children. There should, however, be scope for them to develop a view of what they expect and hope to achieve in mathematics and to understand why the subject is relevant to them. Rose (1998) describes ways in which children can participate in the management of their own learning. He notes that there are a number of reasons cited for not including children in assessment and learning procedures.

Among these reasons is a concern that allowing children to express their views on their learning would undermine the authority of the teacher, particularly when that teacher feels personally challenged by those with learning difficulties. Yet Rose gives evidence of pupil participation overcoming negative attitudes towards schooling and suggests that children who are actively involved in planning and evaluating their education gain in self-esteem and show improvement in communication skills and behaviour. From this we can expect them to feel greater motivation and thus to maintain that we should not allow the mathematics curriculum to be narrowed down into a set of utilitarian exercises aimed solely at developing functional skills. The richness of mathematics can and should be experienced by all pupils.

We will now propose a set of principles that will give shape to the idea of 'inclusive mathematics'.

Inclusive Mathematics

A mathematics curriculum that encompasses the *needs, expectations* and *aspirations* of all pupils, that *motivates* them and *enriches* their school experience.

All pupils in primary education, without exception, will:

- experience a broad and rich mathematical education
- be expected to do better than their perceived best
- participate in projects and initiatives aimed at improving the teaching and learning of mathematics
- benefit from a flexible approach
- have their achievements celebrated
- benefit from their teachers having the confidence to identify their own strengths and weaknesses in teaching mathematics
- experience a dynamic, not restricted, approach to teaching
- experience mathematics as an international language and use it as an effective means of communication with people beyond the school
- benefit from an active commitment within the school and beyond that everyone is entitled to enjoy success in mathematics.

Such principles generate a set of learning goals that can only be achieved through a commitment and determination to do the best for every child. It calls for imagination and a high level of professionalism. This professionalism extends beyond the classroom teacher and includes all adults who are working with them in the classroom. Learning support assistants have a key role in promoting learning even if their work is not generally described as 'teaching'.

To be a successful teacher one has to possess an in-depth knowledge of the content of the curriculum and an understanding of how children learn. Teachers need to be trained for their role and all children are entitled to be taught by a properly trained teacher.

There are, however, a number of ways in which non-teachers can play an effective part in educating children, but they also need adequate preparation as the balance of their role shifts from caring to educating. A booklet by Aplin (1998), written to support the UK National Numeracy Project, gives practical guidance for learning assistants and this topic will be covered in more detail in Chapter 10.

TALKING POINTS

Why is mathematics important for our pupils?
What mathematics do our pupils use in other subjects?

2

The process of mathematical learning – and what can go wrong

Everything that is, I know it.
If I don't, it isn't knowledge.

(Anon)

MATHEMATICS – TAUGHT OR LEARNED?

No such claim could possibly be taken seriously today. If the school curriculum is the means by which the younger generation is introduced to mankind's accumulated knowledge then the information explosion has made it impossible for anyone to possess more than a fragment. Within that rapidly increasing knowledge base is a greater understanding of the way we learn.

Faced with coming to terms with new additional content in the school curriculum, teachers have been left with little time to keep up to date on the advances that have been made in understanding the way the brain works. Having covered the broad range of content in Chapter 1, we now move on to outline some influential views on the process of learning mathematics and consider why some children have difficulty in learning what we think they should.

Public opinion has played an increasingly significant role in recent years in deciding what should be in the school curriculum and how it should be taught. Many of the criticisms made of the current teaching of mathematics are based on adults' memories of how it was taught to them. There has been a presumption that the main task of the teacher is to present a body of knowledge and techniques for solving problems. This patently does not work with every pupil or we would not have any children failing to reach the required standard.

It is therefore necessary to consider why some children do not succeed and whether this places them apart from other children in the way they should be taught. Do they just need some more of the same or do they suffer from a disorder that prevents them from acquiring mathematical ideas?

The notion that young babies were passive recipients of experiences has been exploded by, amongst others, Bower (1977), who showed them to be active participants in learning. Young babies who for some genetic, perinatal or environmental reason lack the capacity or opportunity to have meaningful interaction with their environment and with other people are going to be at a disadvantage in their cognitive development. This will include an underdevelopment of the skill of numerosity, or the ability to recognize number values, and in the development of the vocabulary that will enable them to understand and communicate mathematical ideas.

Children with certain types of physical, sensory and psychological disorders face characteristic difficulties in learning. Whether they suffer from a general lack of ability or damage to a key part of the brain is a matter for the specialist literature and is beyond the scope of this book. For our present purposes, it is sufficient to recognize that there are some children who seem to lack the most fundamental understanding of mathematics. Undoubtedly, a child who has significant physical or sensory problems, and particularly those with a combination of disabilities, will begin at a great disadvantage. If that child is to make educational progress he or she will require the support of skilled specialists from the disciplines of health and education.

Even milder conditions can result in limited achievement and Gulliford and Upton (1992) described characteristic learning difficulties associated with particular types of special educational need. This does not, however, justify the standpoint that certain types of disorder inevitably result in those learning difficulties. It is more in keeping with the principles of inclusion to put aside for the time being the idea that failure in mathematics is the result of some irreversible defect in the child. It would be more productive to look at the process of learning mathematics to see if we can identify where that process most commonly breaks down. Armed with this knowledge we will consider in the second part of this book how the teacher can prepare for the possibility of a child coming up against a problem and introduce strategies to prevent difficulties arising.

HOW CHILDREN LEARN MATHEMATICS

As Matthews (1990) has demonstrated in his work on early mathematical experiences, a lot of mathematical learning takes place before children enter formal education. Some children start school with well-developed skills built on a sound foundation of experience provided by parents, siblings and by the staff of nursery schools or kindergartens. Others will have a jumbled set of specific, semi-formed and probably unrelated bits of learning seasoned with quite fundamental misconceptions. Some will be given the encouraging label 'good at maths', others will be identified by less complimentary epithets.

Mathematics in particular is built on previous learning, and certain key elements of knowledge and skill are prerequisites to successful new learning. Piaget (1952) claimed that children learned these concepts when they were mentally ready to grasp them. He believed that they learned them through experience and that the learning of these concepts cannot be hastened. This line of thought influenced a generation of teachers and led to what has been termed 'discovery learning'. The effect of this was to discourage teachers from directly teaching skills and led them instead to provide opportunities for children to work out mathematical relationships from practical experience. Whilst in practice teachers may not have gone as far down the road of avoiding repetitive learning of number facts as has been claimed by critics, it certainly placed them in a dilemma when faced with children who were not making progress. One outcome was the growth of an alternative mathematics curriculum, which will be considered in Chapter 4.

Donaldson (1978) recognizes that the work of Piaget made a fundamental contribution to our understanding of how children learn basic mathematical concepts but questions whether he was right in his claim that learning could not be hastened. Many teachers, when faced with pupils who do not possess these concepts in any useful way, have felt a professional obligation to employ strategies to enable them to understand and be able to apply these essential tools. This is one example of the tensions that have been created for teachers who know that it is unrealistic to push their pupils towards unachievable targets and yearn for a more suitable approach to mathematics teaching.

WHEN DO WE BEGIN TO LEARN MATHEMATICS?

'Children begin to absorb mathematical ideas from a very early age', stated Matthews (1990). Piaget (1952) set out a detailed account of the stages of intellectual development through which a child passes in developing mathematical concepts. His theories, which are clearly described by Beard (1969), have been extremely influential and have formed the basis for many early mathematical programmes. He believed that children at around 5 years of age arrive at a stage of Number Readiness before which it is not appropriate to teach them mathematics. This pattern of reasoning survives in the National Curriculum, where Level 1 is considered a reasonable expectation for 5-year-olds and anyone not achieving that is considered to be 'working towards'.

A number of writers, most notably Donaldson (1978), have accepted the value of Piaget's theories in giving us a map of the process of learning mathematics. They have, however, challenged a number of key features of that theory. Donaldson believes that Piaget underestimated the understanding of young children and demonstrated this with tasks that were set in contexts meaningful to the children being assessed. The work of Bower (1977) mentioned earlier is an example of how the frontiers of knowledge regarding learning are being extended nearer to birth and should encourage us to recognize the importance of early intervention to promote active learning in young children.

Although Piaget did not specify any teaching methodology, his theories were taken as justification for what was popularly known as discovery learning. This was seen as giving children the opportunity to discover mathematical rules and conventions through exploring patterns and it involved considerably more practical activity than so-called traditional methods. It was presented as the opposite to Rote Learning, where children learned mathematical facts by heart and solved equations according to rules without any real understanding of the processes involved. The inability of some children to repeat multiplication tables was used as a stick with which to beat teachers who had, in popular mythology, abandoned proven methods of instruction in favour of undemanding 'modern methods'. This 'trendiness' was seen as leading to the failure of schools to give children a 'proper education' and became the justification for a concerted attack on teachers and schools that culminated in the 1988 Education Reform Act.

Griffiths (1999) gives a fuller account of the changes that have occurred in mathematics education during the past century in the UK and relates them to the political influences that have led to different priorities being pursued at different times. He regrets the termination of two initiatives, LAMP (Low Attainers in Mathematics Project) and RAMP (Raising Achievement in Mathematics Project), which had in common the collaboration of teachers in curriculum development. This, and similar work of the now defunct Schools Council, was curtailed and replaced by the top-down imposition of the National Curriculum. Politicians took this route as the outcomes of development arising from teachers working together were seen as failing to deliver the required improvement in standards. The most recent example in the UK of curriculum by diktat is the National Numeracy Strategy (DfEE, 1999) which will be referred to in later chapters.

The main outcome of the RAMP project in the present context was the recognition that low attainment in mathematics was not a fixed state but one that could be affected by suitable teaching. This is one in a number of studies demonstrating that, in the currently popular phrase, 'schools can make a difference'. It is therefore reasonable to assume that many children could move from being low attainers if their schools had a positive attitude towards them and the staff were equipped with the strategies to teach them successfully.

HOW THE PROCESS CAN BREAK DOWN

Three kinds of mathematical difficulty have been identified by Strang and Rourke (1985). One is where the child has difficulty in memorizing and retrieving arithmetical facts and tables. Another is the difficulty in following mathematical procedures, associated with a delay in learning basic number skills. The last manifests itself as a difficulty in representing and interpreting arithmetical information.

Teachers will be able to identify children in their class with one or more of these difficulties. However, it must be recognized that the ability to learn and use mathematical skills depends upon a range of mental processes and it is unlikely that one particular difficulty can be related to the breakdown of a single cognitive process (Aubrey, 1998). The complexity of factors extend beyond the child's own internal mental processes and include the conditions in which a child's learning takes place. The question is not whether the child's conditions cause the problem but rather how the influences of home and school interact with and contribute to the child's cognitive growth.

Denvir (Denvir *et al.*, 1982) in her account of the LAMP project gives a list of factors most frequently associated with low attainment. These include:

> physical, physiological or sensory defects; emotional or behavioural problems; impaired performance due to physical causes, such as tiredness, drugs, general ill-health; attitude, anxiety, lack of motivation; inappropriate teaching; too many changes of teachers, lack of continuity; general slowness in grasping ideas; cultural differences, English not first language; impoverished home background; difficulty in expression or in written work; poor reading ability; gaps in education, absence from school, frequent changes of school; immaturity, late development, youngest in year group; low self-concept leading to lack of confidence.

This list reflects characteristics that are not exclusive to low attainment in mathematics. It contains both within-child items and ones that relate to the social and educational context within which the child grows up. In-child factors undoubtedly play a part in hindering normal cognitive development and disabling conditions might themselves be immutable to change given the present state of medical and psychological knowledge. Some can be alleviated by technology, as has been dramatically demonstrated by celebrated cases of people with severely physically disabling conditions. Similarly, science fiction is rapidly becoming fact and the technological enhancement of poor vision, as in *Star Trek*, may well be realized by the time this book is read!

Impediments to learning that relate to the child's social and domestic life can be changed, through cooperation between school, parents and other professions, and the impact on a child's performance of having a healthy diet and a good, undisturbed night's sleep can be quite dramatic. The involvement of parents in activities that enhance the quality of communication with their children can again have beneficial effects on achievement.

Ahmed (1989) looks beyond in-child factors and considers how schools create conditions in which children fail, drawing upon the work of Holt (1969). He believed that many secondary schools did pupils a disservice by:

focusing on the failure of the pupil
believing that a good staff–pupil ratio is the answer to slow learning
having lower pupil expectations
having lower teacher expectations
having lower parent expectations
using methods of teaching which lead to fear of failure.

Teachers in primary education might consider whether this critique is relevant in their situation. Certainly the findings of the LAMP project (Denvir *et al.*, 1982) that there are factors relevant to low attainment which are in the control of the school highlights issues that will apply to a greater or lesser extent in most schools. These factors include:

- inappropriate teaching methods or content
- lack of suitable materials
- lack of responsiveness to the pupil's problems
- lack of teacher's time to reflect on the pupil's difficulties and plan suitable work
- a teacher's lack of detailed knowledge of the mathematics being taught, including a knowledge of which skills, concepts, etc. are involved.

These findings have been available for some time and yet the lessons do not appear to have been universally applied. A report on the teaching of Number in primary schools (Ofsted, 1997) shows that these shortcomings persisted into the 1990s.

The National Numeracy Project was established in England and Wales as a means of tackling the issues that arose from this and similar findings from other studies. An evaluation of schools involved in the first cohort (Ofsted, 1998) showed that improvements in the way teachers planned, organized and carried out the teaching of mathematics led to significant gains by children with SEN. High teacher turnover was recognized as having a negative impact on the consistency of teaching.

The conclusions to be drawn from this report are that improvement in schools depends upon maintaining teaching of a high calibre; having the commitment and sustained interest of the head teacher; and having enthusiastic mathematics coordinators who provide a good role model for colleagues.

LEARNING AND UNDERSTANDING

Teachers' lack of knowledge on how children learn mathematics is cited as a factor in low attainment. Unless they have some knowledge of the process by which children learn mathematics and the place of individual competencies in that process, they might not be able to provide an appropriate progression of learning activities. For example, they need to be able to distinguish between the ability to recite numerals and number facts and the competence to select and use those facts in solving problems.

Skemp (1971) distinguished between 'understanding' and 'learning without understanding'. He illustrates it as the difference between two people finding their way around a town. One has a sketchy plan, the other an accurate mental map of the town. The first one will be lost if he takes one wrong step, the other will be able to construct a route from wherever he starts and adapt that route as he proceeds.

Teachers of children with learning difficulties will be familiar with the child who, after a great deal of explanation and help, appears to have grasped the idea, only to forget it when it comes to solving a new problem to which that knowledge could be applied. There seems to be a breakdown in the ability to transfer learning to unfamiliar situations and this makes it difficult for the teacher to set tasks that the child will be able to solve alone or in a group with children of similar ability. This limitation can result in the child being set repetitive tasks.

The writer experienced this when first encountering children in one of the new special schools arising from the 1970 Education Act in the UK which brought all children under the umbrella of the education service. Classrooms were stocked with attractively produced wooden formboards that were given to the children each day. The parts of the puzzle were removed by the adult working with them, the children replaced the parts with help, the board was put away and another one given to them. The interest and motivation were there, generally, but the whole exercise lacked any progression. No one appeared to have thought that the solving of one problem could be the jumping-off point for tackling a more difficult one, or of building progressive amounts of difficulty into fitting the pieces back in the board. It was as if there was a glass ceiling on what could be expected of the child.

Hatch (1999) quotes some Hungarian teachers who felt that British teachers put more emphasis than they would on safeguarding children's self-image rather than, in their words, 'forcing them to achieve better results'. Allowing for the possibility of non-native English-speakers not appreciating that the word 'forcing' might be open to an interpretation that many teachers would find unacceptable, there is still an indication of a different approach to classroom teaching.

Sharpe (1993) describes a lesson for 7-year-olds that she observed in a primary school in Hungary. The teacher stood at the front and was instructing the children in the use of the Soroban, a type of abacus. The intention was that by physically manipulating the beads the children would learn to calculate by visualizing the movement of the beads. The lesson continued with the children writing sums on their individual chalkboard and holding them up for the teacher to see. She observed that those who got the sums wrong did not seem perturbed. It could be argued that sensitivity to a child's self-esteem might lead to low expectations which might in turn be associated with the relative failure of some children. On the other hand, there is the experience of Rhydderch-Evans (1989), who reports having felt extremely disturbed at the prospect of getting an answer wrong. She contends that the mathematics teaching she received had a negative effect on her self-esteem and led to her giving up the subject at the earliest opportunity.

This difference could be explained by the style of the teacher but it does seem to exemplify a different approach to mathematical education. Sharpe also noted that all Hungarian student teachers spent five hours each week improving their own mathematics as well as learning about teaching mathematics. By knowing the subject, they have the facility to look beyond 'right or wrong' and understand the errors made by the children. This enables them to retrace the steps of learning and consolidate the skills that the child has not yet mastered in smaller ability-grouped sessions between the whole-class teaching sessions. It might also have maintained in them a constant awareness of the feelings that might be prompted by giving an incorrect answer. From the evidence of observing lessons in primary and special schools in Hungary there appears to be a general application of the principle that incorrect answers are not wrong answers but steps towards a correct solution.

This approach is being promoted in the UK with the Numeracy Strategy (DfEE, 1999). One of the key components of Hungarian mathematics lessons is the considerable amount of time devoted to teaching the whole class. There is a fear that some children will not be able to keep up with the lesson and thus become marginalized. This will certainly need to be monitored carefully if teachers are to avoid a fresh outbreak of 'maths phobia'. In later chapters we will see how some teachers are dealing with this issue.

Here again, we must be aware that the solution could be more damaging than the problem. If the model is adapted to accommodate the traditional view of children with SEN needing 'something different', we will return to a situation where those children receive alternative 'whole-class lessons'. This will make it difficult to evaluate whether a full mixed-ability grouping, with a 'no blame, no shame' style of teaching might have been more effective for them or might indeed have led to a lower incidence of low attainment.

Teachers are rightly aware that it is unrealistic to expect all children to keep up with the more capable ones in the class. Whilst some will respond to the challenge, there will be one or two in a mixed-ability primary class who do not. O'Toole and O'Toole (1989) set tests for 7-year-olds based upon examples given by the UK's National Curriculum subject working group. They found that many of the 7-year-olds were unable to succeed at Level 1 in the Mathematics National Curriculum whereas Levels 2 or 3 would be the normal expectation.

Typical assessment tasks for Level 1 involved counting how many objects there were in a set of up to ten objects and answering questions on subtraction from ten. Children in a school for pupils with moderate learning difficulties (MLD) were working on the attainment targets at Level 1 but did not answer enough of the questions in the test to achieve that level. Children in a severe learning difficulties (SLD) school were not achieving even the lowest statement of attainment in Level 1.

WHY DO SOME CHILDREN HAVE DIFFICULTY WITH MATHEMATICS?

Many explanations have been given for low mathematical achievement. For a large number it may be part of a general difficulty in learning that has resulted from the factors described by Denvir. These might be inherent in the child, having occurred as the result of damage to the central nervous system during birth or as a result of an accident. They could be the legacy of inappropriate teaching at some time during the child's education. In some instances, the roots may lie in a combination of these factors.

Other children may appear to have a normal level of ability but suffer a 'block' in specific areas. Chinn and Ashcroft (1996) describe the anxieties that children with dyslexia bring to their mathematics lessons. Many will have developed idiosyncratic methods for solving problems and will have important gaps in their knowledge. The authors recognize the need to give them the structure they lack without denying them a breadth of mathematical experiences.

The difficulties in language acquisition that are associated with impaired hearing (Fraser, 1992) will affect the child's ability to develop mathematical concepts as these invariably depend upon understanding and responding to vocabulary used in a specific way. Children who are deaf have difficulty in participating in interactive teaching sessions, particularly those who need signing support. Whilst such support does enable them to follow the main topic, it is hard for them to be involved in the dynamics of the lesson. They are not always aware of the asides and comments that are present in an active classroom and the time lag between understanding and responding means that the rest of the class will have moved on to a fresh idea. This will apply to a greater or lesser degree depending upon the severity of the hearing loss, but even a relatively minor loss in early childhood can have an effect on language, and therefore concept, development.

Visual impairment can result in difficulties at the early stages of learning mathematics when poor hand/eye coordination presents difficulties in practical tasks. When, at a later stage, children are required to produce written answers there are likely to be errors in recording their answers. As Mason (1995) points out, they will have difficulty in reading poor quality worksheets and processing information presented in a non-linear manner.

Children with learning difficulties will present a range of specific difficulties as well as a generally low level of attainment in mathematics. Mild or moderate learning difficulties are often associated with differing combinations of the factors in Denvir's list referred to earlier in this chapter. Those with Down's syndrome have difficulty in receiving and processing auditory information and rely on visual input (Lorenz, 1999).

The result is that some children have fundamental misconceptions or a lack of confidence which, when corrected, enable them to achieve within the normal range. Such children are often considered for return to mainstream education. Teachers in special schools have anecdotal evidence of children whose progress has been so marked that, with self-esteem re-established, they are reintegrated successfully. In the writer's own experience, a boy returned to a secondary school which setted by ability for mathematics and very soon moved from the low attainers set into a higher one.

At the other end of the spectrum will be children who, nearing the end of compulsory education, are still struggling with basic mathematics at the infant level. Within the range are children who are making limited progress. They can sort objects by one or more attributes — for example, they can select 'the large, green triangle' (three attributes) from a collection of mixed shapes. They can count and add within the range 1–10 and even 1–100 but appear to have difficulty when presented with an unfamiliar problem that calls upon those skills. It has to be said, though, that they often show a greater facility in solving those problems when they are faced with a problem that they find highly motivating.

Children with physical disabilities can experience some or all of the difficulties described, depending upon the nature and severity of their disorder. To make generalizations about the impact of special educational needs learning difficulties on learning mathematics is therefore to become embroiled in contradictions. Profiles of assessment of the various strands of the mathematical curriculum often show a jagged pattern rather than the smoother one of children who are making normal progress.

The more severe the learning difficulties the more marked is the discrepancy between minimal and normal progress. Mathematics might not seem to be a high priority for children with profound and multiple learning difficulties. Many teachers would argue that their curriculum should be geared towards awareness and self-help rather than subject-specific targets. However, the argument about the need to provide opportunity for those with severe learning difficulties so that they can demonstrate unexpected skills is still valid.

TALKING POINTS

What problems do children in my class have with mathematics?
Are they in-child factors or do they result from something we do in school?

3

The challenge for teachers – an international view

Our future prosperity depends on investment in education, and maths is a key subject which should not be neglected.

(Burghes, 1996)

STANDARDS

Teachers find themselves at the centre of an ongoing international debate on school effectiveness. It usually centres around 'standards' and comparisons are drawn between the relative ease with which children of a particular age in different countries can handle complex numerical problems. Aubrey (1998) shows that there are inconsistencies in such comparisons. For example, she found when comparing English and Slovene 8-year-olds that the English children were ahead in problem-solving but the Slovene children excelled in arithmetic. There are also indications that proportionally more children in England are at risk of low achievement.

Mailhos *et al.* (1996) report on the higher levels achieved by Hungarian primary school children and describe how teachers in training from Hungary, France and England reacted on observing lessons in each country. One English student was in favour of introducing the didactic Hungarian approach into English schools, as has subsequently happened with the National Numeracy Strategy (DfEE, 1999). On the other hand, several Hungarian teachers showed great interest in the more reflective style they observed in English schools.

During their visit to Hungary the student teachers visited a school that specialized in mathematics. Overall the standards achieved by most of the children were probably two years in advance of those of their English counterparts but each year up to 5 per cent of children were held back a year because they did not achieve the required standard. This illustrates a key aspect of the standards debate: a standard that everyone reaches is worthless. Whatever philosophical stance is taken, a standard, to have any degree of public acceptance, has to be too challenging for some, but not for too many. This brings us back once more to a cohort of children, between 2 and 20 per cent, who are not included in the aspirations and expectations of the majority of children, of their parents and of the society in which they live.

INVESTING IN THE LOW ATTAINER

In an age of cost-effectiveness there will be those who question whether it is worth using scarce resources to improve the achievement of all children. Would it not be better to 'back the winners' and make sure that our brightest young people are given the concentrated attention that is devoted to those with special needs?

The philosophical and principled arguments against this view have been well rehearsed, although Jacobson (1999) does challenge the accepted wisdom of allocating a disproportionate level of resources to some groups of pupils. If we consider the argument in relation to a country's standing in the world then international comparisons of mathematical achievement show that most countries educate their prosperous middle-class children to about the same level (Burkhardt, 1999). The low standing of Britain and the USA in comparative tables is due to the poor achievement of the less-advantaged pupils, who figure prominently in the group we would identify as low attainers. As a group of teachers in Ireland pointed out, if a child is brought up in a family whose members have limited numeracy, it follows that they will not receive the pre-school experiences that would support the development of mathematical skills and concepts. In the Hungarian study described earlier, it was noted that those who failed to achieve the required standard received after-school tuition in their weak subjects.

It would seem, therefore, that the raising of standards for the lowest-attaining pupils is in the national and not just the individual interest. The British government includes children with special needs in its strategy to raise educational standards (DfEE, 1997) and the intention of the National Numeracy Strategy (DfEE, 1999) is to provide a structure to help *all* children achieve their potential.

CONTROL OF MATHEMATICS TEACHING

Whatever one's view of the process by which children learn, or fail to learn, mathematics, teaching is now governed in many countries by nationally defined guidelines. They set out the pattern for progression and often state clear expectations for each age or phase of schooling. The Dutch work to a series of minimum educational goals and the recently launched Irish curriculum defines the content of mathematics teaching for each age group in primary schools.

Some countries go further and make statements on how mathematics should be taught. The *Non-Statutory Guidance to the Mathematics National Curriculum for England and Wales* (DES, 1989) gave the following guidelines for a scheme of work in mathematics:

- Activities should bring together different areas of mathematics.
- Activities should be a balance between tasks that develop knowledge, skills and understanding, and those that develop the ability to tackle practical problems.
- Activities should be balanced between different modes of learning: doing, observing, talking, and listening, discussing with other pupils, reflecting, drafting, reading and writing, etc.
- Activities should enable pupils to develop a positive attitude to mathematics.

The Numeracy Strategy (DfEE, 1999) goes beyond prescribing the content of the mathematics curriculum and promotes a whole-class interactive teaching approach. The justification given for taking this position is the consensus between American and British research, the British professional knowledge base and the findings of comparative international studies that this approach results in effective teaching (Muijs, 1999).

Schools are expected to make detailed termly programmes for each age group based on the format set out in the framework. Each lesson consists of three parts: a whole-class introductory session, followed by group work and ending with a whole-class plenary session. There is recognition that some children will need additional support to keep pace with the lesson but the emphasis is on retaining all the children in the class rather than some being taken elsewhere for separate lessons.

A Dutch colleague reports a similar approach in his school. He describes a typical mathematics lesson in the primary school where he is special educational needs coordinator: 'The lesson begins with the children being given instructions, then they work independently. This gives the teacher more time for the children with SEN. There might also be another teacher working in the classroom' (the school has a special needs support teacher as well as the special needs coordinator).

He confirms that teachers are expected to include children with SEN in their lessons. As he says, 'This means more adaptation in their daily organization.' He once recounted to the writer his experience during seven years as special needs coordinator:

> At first teachers expected me to remove the children with special needs from their class. After staff training and support from myself and the school's remedial teacher things have changed. They now ask what they need to do to educate the child in their class.

The successful teaching of children who have difficulties in mathematics requires a complex range of skills on the part of the teacher and, as the example above shows, the school's SENCO has a major part to play in developing the capabilities of colleagues.

It is certainly true that many teachers are feeling more confident at incorporating a wider range of needs in their classes, as long as they have adequate support. But as inclusion encompasses children with more complex needs who would previously have been placed in special schools, teachers in primary schools find the prospect of trying to engage all children in their mathematics lessons a daunting one.

It also presents a challenge to those charged with drawing up curriculum guidelines, whether informal or formal. To make them sufficiently broad to encompass the likely achievements of even the lowest-achieving child is to face the prospect of being accused of lowering standards. Understandably, there is a fear that to state those very basic learning targets in the context of education for older primary and secondary children is to be seen as condoning low expectations. The alternative is to set expectations, or targets, for children at particular ages and to say that the majority of children are expected to achieve that target. Doing so immediately excludes those who will not. Even a target that expresses a progressively larger proportion of children achieving it will still depend for its validity on there being some who will not, otherwise it will be condemned as meaningless.

The statements of attainment for each level in the British National Curriculum began as grade criteria but soon became regarded as norms. For example, one of the criteria for Level 3 was that children could 'demonstrate that they know and can use their multiplication tables'. Levels 2 and 3 were intended to describe the average and above-average range of achievement for 7-year-olds, with all of them being expected to have achieved Level 1. As the results of National Curriculum tests for 7-year-olds became public, articles appeared in the popular media that included comments along the lines of 'all 7-year-olds should know their tables' and criticizing schools where inspectors had found otherwise.

RESPONDING TO DIVERSITY

The challenge for the teacher, whether in an inclusive classroom, in a streamed class or in a special school, is that not all children achieve appropriate levels. The streamed classroom will probably contain the narrowest spread of attainment and there are indications that ability grouping will be one of the outcomes of the UK Numeracy Strategy. Such systems are, according to Sebba and Ainscow (1996), 'largely incompatible with developing inclusion'.

Even where all the low-attaining children are grouped together, leaving aside for the present whether that is anti-inclusive, the teacher will still have to cater for a wide range of needs and learning characteristics. Presumably this would be the group where children who needed regular individual support would be placed. Assuming therefore that those who needed additional support would also be present, then we begin to see the magnitude of the teacher's task.

In order to cater for the diversity of needs and learning styles within their class they will require a range of approaches and, ideally, the presence of an additional adult to make it possible to maintain support for those who need additional support. It will be essential for those who need regular individual support that there is an additional teacher or a trained learning support assistant.

One of the teacher's concerns will be the current thinking on appropriate methodology. Longer-serving teachers will have experienced changes in what is and what is not acceptable in mathematics teaching. Maths schemes that were at one time highly recommended are no longer acceptable. At one time infant teachers were being encouraged to allow their pupils to use calculators, now their use is officially discouraged (DfEE, 1999).

There has been a view that the use of structural apparatus, such as Stern and Dienes, should be discontinued once children have reached a certain age. It would appear sensible to be less rigid and allow children to use them until their mental structures have become well established.

CHANGES IN MATHEMATICS EDUCATION

The teaching of mathematics has undergone considerable changes in recent years. Daniels and Anghileri (1995) give an account of the changes that have taken place in secondary mathematics and these are mirrored in primary education.

Looking to the future, Higginson (1999) sees mathematics teaching moving from a mechanistic style to one that embraces creativity and imagination and give pupils the opportunity to refine their knowledge with the guidance of a skilled teacher. He envisages classroom mathematics that 'is embedded in potentially-rich learning situations that are interesting and relevant for students and enable all to participate and grow'. He describes three Canadian projects, one of which has strong artistic links.

Such a view of mathematics teaching is far removed from the turgid diet of worksheets that were the lot of many low-attaining pupils. Hatch (1999) believes that there are two basic teacher assumptions that have to be questioned. Firstly, there is the importance of getting right answers, the overwhelming 'turn-off' for Rhydderch-Evans (1989). Secondly, there is the assumption that the main task of a teacher is to explain.

The RAMP and LAMP projects brought a fresh perspective to the problem but unfortunately much of that has been submerged beneath the welter of new initiatives. Ahmed (1989) believes that they had two major outcomes; low achievers have been able to achieve more in mathematics than they could previously and teachers have been able to revise their ideas about mathematics and have changed their classroom methods. He contends that the findings of these projects and the supporting publications make a vital contribution to the principle of 'Access' as outlined at the beginning of the revised *Mathematics in the National Curriculum* document (DfE, 1995) that followed the Dearing Report (SCAA, 1994).

ACCESS, SUPPORT AND DEPENDENCY

The word 'access' at the primary as well as secondary phase of education has a broader meaning than facilities to overcome physical or sensory disabilities. In its wider sense it refers to children's cognitive preparedness for work related to the mathematics they encounter when beginning formal education. It also carries the implication that someone other than the child is taking action to make learning accessible. As Evans (1997) has pointed out, 'the greater the learning difficulty a child is experiencing, the more the teacher must act as a mediator between the child and his environment to compensate for these difficulties.' The principle of access to learning therefore places an onus on schools to take positive action in response to children's needs and not to regard those needs as barriers to participation.

A distinction has to be drawn between support and dependency. In the particular instance of a child receiving regular individual support it is essential that the adult does not take over. Thomas *et al.* (1998) give examples of where children have allowed the adult to make responses or requests on their behalf when, with support or carefully judged questioning, they might have been able to do it themselves. In other cases, children have refused support because they see it as separating them from the norms of the class.

In a more general sense, Hatch (1999) believes that children begin schooling with the ability to work creatively in mathematics but lose it, largely due to teacher behaviour and expectations, with the result that they become dependent learners. In her observation of teachers she saw examples of an approach based on the idea that children had to be instructed on how to respond to each new kind of problem rather than being led to finding their own solution.

This is supported by Cockburn's (1999) view that the busy teacher might not consider how a pupil's imagination or creativity will have contributed to an answer that is wrong in terms of mathematical correctness but makes sense in everyday terms. She contends that children on entering school soon learn to play the 'mathematics game' where the imperative is to find the right answer, much as teachers might like to think that they are emphasizing the process rather than the product.

HIGH-ENERGY LEARNING

Hatch (1999) believes that the role of the teacher should be to keep all children in a 'high-energy state' throughout their mathematical learning. She recognizes the difficulties that might arise with less-able children but still regards it as a priority that children give a logical explanation of the mathematics they are doing. An example that comes to mind is of an 8-year-old girl with Down's syndrome when presented with a problem that involved placing reels on circles drawn on a card. The exercise was in one-to-one correspondence and when presented with the correct number of reels (four) she placed them without difficulty. When presented with five she looked quizzically at the teacher, who assumed that she could not solve the problem and was ready to tick the 'Working towards' box in the assessment sheet. The teacher decided to prompt a response and asked her to try to place them. Once again the girl looked at the teacher, then said 'I can't.'

When asked why not, she explained. 'Look, this one has got somewhere to sit [placing one reel on a circle], and this one, and this one, and this one, but [picking up the fifth reel] this one has got nowhere to sit.' What appeared to be a lack of ability to complete the task proved to be a recognition that it was not solvable in the way the teacher had asked. Far from 'working towards', she was one step ahead!

TIME FOR PLANNING

The teacher is expected to organize the classroom so that the work of every child can be managed. Inclusion, by extending the range of individual learning characteristics present in the class, inevitably adds a further dimension to the teacher's task. It may be creating opportunities to work with every child, it may be managing the work of learning support assistants, it may be collaborating with a specialist teacher; it may well involve all three. This represents a significant shift from the traditional role of the class teacher.

Such a variety of demands can only be handled by sound planning. The customary response to children with SEN has been to make special arrangements as a variation on what had been planned for the class. Inclusive mathematics requires those individual adaptations to be considered at the planning stage.

Curriculum planning can no longer be a case of following the same syllabus each year. One is reminded of the comment about the long-serving teacher who, it was suggested, had not been teaching mathematics for 30 years but had repeated the same year's teaching 30 times! Today's teachers know that to be away from school for any length of time means a lot of catching up on the changes that have taken place.

School inspectors will expect to see evidence that the teacher has planned what is to be covered in the school year, has a clear idea of what the children will be expected to learn each term and has detailed teaching plans for each week. The tasks of support staff and the input of specialist teachers and other professionals, such as speech therapists and physiotherapists, will be expected to figure in those plans.

In order to draw up effective plans, teachers will need time to meet with the various people with whom they will be collaborating. Time is probably the scarcest resource in any school and the head teacher has a responsibility to build into the school year time for planning and reviewing work. This will mean making some very difficult choices in terms of the priority given to the various demands upon the time of teachers and support staff.

Visiting teachers work to a tight schedule and releasing a teacher from the classroom to meet with them will require someone else to teach the class. It can be, however, time very well spent. The introduction of the National Curriculum led to many subject advisory teachers being involved with special schools in Britain for the first time. The synergy created by subject specialists working with teachers in special education led to both having to rethink their approaches and did much to enrich the curriculum in those schools. More recently, the involvement of special schools in the National Numeracy Project has had a similar effect.

PLANNING TEACHING

The Framework for Numeracy (DfEE, 1999) proposes that prior to the lesson the teacher should have worked out the following:

● *Topics to be covered in the opening whole-class session.*
  The Framework does allow for the possibility of there being two parallel whole-group sessions taking place in one classroom, particularly in special schools. This may be a practical way of managing the diversity of needs within a class but there is still merit in bringing the whole class together for a short input from

the teacher. It creates a feeling of 'working together' not only for the children but also for the other adults in the classroom.

- *Short tasks for pupils to do in pairs.*
  Children of similar ability who are independent learners can be set a task that can be completed in a limited time. It will be within their capability to undertake without help from the teacher and might well involve the consolidation of previous learning.

- *Activities for more-confident children while the teacher works with the rest of the class.*
  Some children will be ready to tackle a problem independently before the rest of the class and could be set written or practical exercises. By having an activity ready for them the teacher will be able to spend more time working with the rest of the class and it will prevent the more-able children from being frustrated at having to wait for the others. When the majority are ready to work on their own the teacher will then be able to work with those who need additional support. This would also create time to check on the progress of the work being carried out by classroom support staff with the children receiving regular individual support.

- *Open-ended activities which allow responses at different levels.*
  These could be problems, games or puzzles that allow for different levels of response from the children. The teacher will need to have ready a range of resources so that each child has available the materials he/she needs to work on the task. For example, some children may still need structural apparatus as an aid for solving computation problems. At stages during the session they could be paired with children who have established mental structures and do not need this apparatus. Those children could work through their answers with them, using the apparatus as a check on accuracy.

- *Key questions.*
  Experienced teachers know that the questions they ask are as important as the answers they get. They should plan in advance questions that involve every child. This topic will be covered in more detail at a later stage.

- *How pupils will be grouped.*
  The teacher should consider whether groupings should be fixed or varied. For some activities it may be better to group children with a similar level of ability or attainment, for others a child with an incomplete grasp of the mathematics involved might benefit from working with someone who has a better understanding of how to complete the activity.

- *Which group the teacher will work with.*
  It is recommended that the teacher aims to work with every group during a week. The work of the other groups has to be planned. Those groups that will be working independently need to know

where to find resources and what to do if they experience difficulties. They should be able to complete set tasks without adult support and not have to interrupt the teacher. Additional exercises have to be prepared for those who might finish early.

● *Plan allocation of support staff.*
The teacher should ensure that support staff know which children they will be working with and understand the activities they are doing with their groups. Time should be found each day for the support teacher or learning assistant to give feedback to the teacher. This should become an established daily plan–review–plan process.

MANAGING TIME

The process described above, when duplicated for other aspects of the curriculum, represents a significant amount of time and has to be recognized within the school's approach to time management. Knight (1989) gives a comprehensive account of the way in which school time is used and suggests a number of strategies for maximizing available time. He points out that teachers' time can be taken up with activities that do not directly impinge on their teaching. To some extent this is necessary to ensure the smooth running of a school but the time taken should be balanced against the time teachers need to plan adequately.

MANAGING THE CLASSROOM

The image of the teacher standing in front of serried rows of children may be reflected in current thinking on whole-class teaching but deeper analysis of the teacher's role shows a shift from direct instruction to managing learning. In practice this means that the teacher has much more to consider than the transmission of subject matter to a, supposedly, homogeneous group of pupils. It has never actually been like that, for teachers have always been aware of the slow or backward child in the class. The difference is that the teacher is encouraged to take account of those children rather than seek an alternative placement for them.

The challenges teachers face are: to ensure that they are teaching mathematics in a way that includes all the children in the class; that the children find it relevant and meaningful; and that it motivates and challenges, but does not discourage, every child. They will need to know each child's individual learning characteristics and use their own skills and imagination to cater for them. They will be aiming for all children to develop their own 'mental maps' so that they can use the skills they possess to deal with new challenges. As we have seen, their own experience of being taught mathematics may have left them with a negative view of the subject and this issue will be addressed in Chapter 13.

To support them in this task teachers can draw upon published resources, of which there is a proliferation. Educational exhibitions, like the annual Education Show in England, are big business and tap into the ability of schools to purchase a wide range of materials to support learning. A broadening of the range of needs in classes often leads to a demand for more resources. These resources, whether purchased, borrowed or made, have to be managed and this can add to the teacher's workload. The latter category is very real for teachers who search the catalogues in vain for something to use with a particular child. Workshop sessions on professional development courses provide a good opportunity for teachers to share ideas and prevent them all having to 'reinvent the wheel'.

TALKING POINTS

How in your school do the class teacher, mathematics co-ordinator and SENCO

- *evaluate whether mathematics teaching is meeting the needs of all pupils?*
- *develop an approach to teaching the whole ability range in a class?*

4

A special mathematics?

Our teaching methods should be so devised that it (number)
can be taught with understanding and continuing success.

(Tansley and Gulliford, 1960)

AN ALTERNATIVE CURRICULUM

We have seen the impact of the work of Piaget and how it encouraged
the development of discovery learning methods. The outcome of
adherence to this philosophy was that some children were unable to
benefit from the type of mathematics teaching they received. Children
with learning difficulties were recognized as having difficulty in
transferring learning from one situation to another and this made it
hard for them to prosper in a learning environment where that was a
key demand. They also had difficulties in recording information in an
acceptable manner and this again disadvantaged them.

One solution was to provide an alternative curriculum. In special
schools this usually meant an individualized approach focusing on
arithmetic and in mainstream schools it sometimes involved removing
children from the class lesson to have remedial teaching, again with a
limited content. They were even further disadvantaged because the
guidance available was extremely limited in comparison to the
techniques available for remedial reading. The usual approach was to
reduce their mathematical experiences. It was felt to be essential that
they could compute and record their answers and much of their time
was spent on this kind of repetitive activity to the neglect of activities
that were seen as 'too difficult'. Again, in contrast to primary teachers'
appreciation of the development of reading, there were few remedial
or special needs support teachers who specialized in mathematics and
the knowledge base was therefore limited.

In a study of the views of a number of writers on the content of a
mathematics curriculum for slow-learning pupils (Robbins, 1981) a
general consensus was found around certain topics: *Number, Fractions,
Money, Measurement, Time, Graphs and Pictorial Representation.*

The following items from the Cockroft foundation list (DES, 1982)
do not relate directly in title but they do have common content items.

Percentages – not mentioned in the former list. They are a different way of expressing fractions and the use of them to express a portion of a whole is perhaps more common now than at the time of publication of the literature referred to for the study. Metrication may have helped to make percentages more readily understandable. For example, it is more usual to say '0.25 metres' than 'a quarter of a metre' and another item on the Cockroft list, Use of Calculators, would also lead to fractions being expressed in a decimal format. This might well result in a reduction in the use of most fractions, except perhaps 'half', which is a commonly used term that occurs in contexts not directly associated with mathematical tasks.

Shape, Sets, Pattern and *Geometry* were the other items arising from the study while the remaining items on the Cockroft list were *Ratio and Proportion, Statistical Ideas* and *Spatial Concepts.* The latter includes the concept of scale in geometrical drawings and maps and can, for our present purposes, be considered to incorporate geometry.

The Cockroft committee drew attention to two aspects of statistics, averages and probability, and set teachers the aim of encouraging a critical attitude to statistics when used by the media.

Ratio and Proportion have practical application in technology and food sciences. Children would also be expected to appreciate direct and inverse variation; for example, the relationship between speed and distance travelled (direct) and speed and time taken to travel a set distance (inverse).

Most, if not all, of these items would be present in a primary mathematics curriculum. The differences between mainstream and special education would be in the pace and level of activity followed with children of a particular age. For Ashdown and Devereux (1990), the mathematics curriculum of a school for pupils with severe learning difficulties would focus on very simple skills and elements of mathematics would only be introduced when they are functional for the individual pupil. Nearly half the pupils in one such school were at a pre-number stage and of the rest the majority were learning numbers up to ten. The main aims for mathematics in this school were:

- learning a meaningful vocabulary related to mathematics
- learning to count
- learning to use numbers
- establishing understanding of the use of the clock, the ruler, the calendar and the thermometer and those measures related to cooking
- learning to recognize coins and notes and their equivalencies and to use money in simple transactions
- understanding and using simple number facts in 'real-life' problem-solving situations.

The Cockroft committee was aware of two dangers in setting out a foundation list. One was that it might encourage a public view that every child would be able to achieve everything on the list. The other danger was that it would be taken as a complete mathematics syllabus for all lower-attaining pupils.

The danger of reduction is also present in the Framework for Numeracy (DfEE, 1999) where certain key objectives are highlighted. Again, it is made clear that they should not be taken as the whole curriculum for some children.

MATHEMATICS FOR LOW ATTAINERS

Reference has been made earlier to the Low Attainers in Mathematics Project (Denvir *et al.*, 1982) which brought another distinct strand into the mainstream mathematics–special mathematics picture. Whilst it was not aimed at pupils with special educational needs, it is clear that the level of support needed by some pupils mentioned would constitute 'additional support' in the terminology adopted for this book.

Ahmed (1996) believes that the Low Attainment in Mathematics Project (LAMP) and the succeeding Raising Achievement in Mathematics Project (RAMP) led to low-attaining pupils achieving more in mathematics than they could previously. He believes that this occurred because of the higher expectations of pupils and of teachers revising their ideas about mathematics and changing their teaching methods. Lewis (1991) accepts that some children have problems in learning mathematics, but the extent to which those difficulties are problematic for the teacher depends upon how the school responds to the child.

It would appear, therefore, that three types of mathematics curricula have developed; the mainstream, with expectations that the majority – 70 per cent is the figure set by the present UK government – will achieve an acceptable standard. The next strand is for the low attainers, where the standards achieved can be raised, as the projects mentioned above have demonstrated. This leaves a third strand, mathematics in special education, which has diverged from normal expectations and has developed into an alternative approach.

The enthusiasm with which many teachers in special education pressed for their pupils to be included in the British National Curriculum was an expression of the reluctance to be sidelined in a major development for the education system. Undoubtedly it created problems in defining appropriate learning targets but it did create a frame of reference against which children's progress could be judged.

It challenged the expectations of teachers in special education and caused them to reconsider the methods of working that had evolved in that sector. A good example was the requirement for pupils to demonstrate the ability to use and apply mathematics. It caused teachers to think about the breadth and relevance of the curriculum they were providing. From that requirement sprang a number of innovatory projects that asked more of the pupils than merely completing page after page of worksheets. The running of two conferences on Interactive Approaches, reported by Smith (1990), reflected a reaction at the time against seeing a child with learning difficulties as a passive recipient of learning and a move towards recognizing their potential to be active participants in their education. Similar sentiments are apparent in the guidance accompanying the Numeracy Strategy (DfEE, 1999).

The following policy statement from a special school for children with learning difficulties illustrates an attempt to relate the school's established approach to mathematics to the requirements of the National Curriculum.

Aims

Entitlement

Each child has an entitlement to the Programmes of Study for Mathematics within the National Curriculum.

Mathematics is an essential means of communication that is used daily by people in all aspects of living.

Mathematics is important in helping children analyse and communicate information and ideas. There is an entitlement for all pupils to a wide range of mathematical experiences that develop each pupil's knowledge, skills and understanding through a broad, balanced, relevant and differentiated curriculum that is designed to meet their immediate and future needs.

Mathematics should be taught to pupils at a level relevant to their developmental age and ability.

Enjoyment

Mathematics should be an enjoyable activity and should be taught through a variety of different experiences from which pupils derive pleasure and enjoyment. It is important to emphasize the effective use of mathematics in a wide range of purposeful tasks that should be set in a manner that challenges pupils and yet gives them the opportunity to succeed.

Relevant

Mathematics should, wherever possible, be made relevant to everyday situations and it is therefore important to help pupils realize the links between the different aspects of mathematics and activities designed to develop skills necessary to lead as independent a lifestyle as possible. Mathematics should be linked with other subjects, and cannot, in this context, be separated from language, which also plays an important part in all areas of the curriculum.

Equal Opportunities
All pupils have an entitlement to equal opportunities in mathematics, irrespective of gender, ethnicity, class or language. Teachers have a responsibility to encourage all pupils to believe in their own ability and reach their own potential. Teachers should be aware of the individual needs of pupils and ensure that the material and examples used are free from gender and racial stereotyping.

Balance
There should be a balance between practical, oral and representational work and pupils should be encouraged to find their own methods for a mathematical task. Pupils should be engaged in activities that have a mathematical content for a minimum of three and a half hours each week. These activities can be taught in a cross-curricular approach and in other subject areas as well as mathematics. Pupils should experience working in a variety of groupings, ranging from one to one, small groups, class teaching or even larger groupings.

Objectives
Mathematics should include the:
  development of factual knowledge
  development of basic mathematical skills
  development of concepts
  development of basic strategies for problem solving
  development of personal skills.

This statement expresses principles that are very similar to those followed in mainstream education. This illustrates how the National Curriculum has provided a common terminology and points of reference for relating the mathematical experiences of the children in special education to those in mainstream schools.

The distinctions occur in the content and method of teaching, as Ashdown and Devereux (1990) show in their description of a mathematics curriculum for children with severe learning difficulties.

'SPECIAL' EDUCATION

What is the 'specialness' of special education? There is evidence, as Aubrey (1993) points out, that the placement of children with SEN does not seem to affect their educational outcomes. It follows from this that we should be more concerned with the process of teaching than where children are taught.

There are specialist teaching principles that apply when children have disabling conditions that prevent them from responding to normal styles of teaching. Whereas children with partial hearing or partial sight might be able to learn from normal teaching approaches, deaf and blind children require alternative means of communication. In Denmark this would probably be provided by a specially trained teacher who would work in the classroom with the class teacher. In the UK teachers or learning support assistants would be available to work with those children at certain times. In Europe in general the most usual form of support is for a specialist teacher to work with the child for between two and four hours each week and also to give support to the class teacher (EADSNE, 1999). This can vary from written guidance to the joint planning of individual learning programmes.

For children with learning difficulties it is much more difficult to discern a specialist body of knowledge. Reynolds (1989) suggests that such children need 'high-density' normal education. This is consistent with the idea that 'high-density' teaching approaches can be incorporated into mainstream methodology. There is, however, a danger that teaching approaches developed in special schools may not travel well. Ainscow (1997) warns against their direct importation into mainstream schools.

APPROACHES TO MATHEMATICS TEACHING FOR PUPILS WITH SEN

The scene in a special school's mathematics lesson would probably be one of children working alone or with a learning support assistant on an individual programme. This programme will probably consist of learning targets broken down into small sub-skills that are deemed to be achievable for the individual child and may differ significantly for those set for another child in the same class. This is in contrast to the common content being taught to a primary school class where whole-class teaching and cooperative group work are likely to be the main modes of curriculum delivery.

The traditional approach for those who cannot keep up with the rest of the class has been to attempt to put right what has gone wrong by setting the children more of the work that they have been finding difficult. Publishers of mathematics schemes have included additional, or alternative, materials for children with learning difficulties. Teachers have bought, or often made, worksheets designed to set tasks in a simpler format, with a controlled vocabulary.

Support for children with special needs in mainstream schools usually targeted literacy. Numeracy rarely figured in the work of peripatetic remedial teachers. The kind of differentiation that occurred usually meant reducing the breadth of the curriculum rather than giving every child a wide range of mathematical experiences. This is understandable in terms of what is relevant and meaningful to children with problems in learning but it does call into question whether, with a little imagination, the interest and fascination shown by the more successful children could not be kindled in every one.

PREVENTING LOW ATTAINMENT

Having considered how we might rescue those children who have failed in mathematics, we will now look at how that failure might be prevented, or at least minimized, by setting a programme that highlights problems before they lead to failure. In doing so we must bear in mind the danger of reducing the risk of failure by removing challenge. Whilst the idea of errorless learning, which involves building knowledge in a series of very small steps so that nothing slips through the net, has its attractions, it may result in the same kind of limited mathematical diet we have referred to previously.

In practice it may be difficult to keep lessons interesting if there is no challenge. A skilled teacher will use the response of the pupils in interactive sessions to guide the development of maths lessons. The incorrect responses are as important, if not more so, in guiding the teacher towards extending the child's knowledge.

A DEVELOPMENTAL APPROACH

Aubrey (1998) suggests that by taking a developmental perspective and drawing upon research on how children normally develop mathematical knowledge much can be discovered about learning difficulties in mathematics. She describes how children adopt strategies to solve problems and then adapt, and sometimes discard, those strategies as they develop more efficient ones.

Problem solving requires the child to move beyond simple practical calculations involving counting objects to performing mental operations on the information before them. For this they require a range of new skills and this proves to be a major stumbling block for children with learning difficulties. The arithmetical skills that they possess have to be used in conjunction with thought processes that rely upon the possession of mental maps, or concepts, which are consistent and logical. They depend upon a secure understanding of words that have a specific meaning in mathematical terms.

Recent developments in the UK are aimed at increasing children's fluency in mental operations and it is suggested that this will be beneficial to all children, including those with SEN (DfEE, 1999). From what Aubrey (1998) has said, it is clear that the appropriate starting place for children with learning difficulties is to ascertain the extent to which they possess the informal mathematical knowledge that most children bring with them when they start school. Whilst the long-term aim might be to have all children working to the same aims, teachers have to accept that building the foundations of mathematical knowledge may involve creating learning experiences to teach skills that most primary school children will have moved beyond. The Mathsteps materials (Robbins, 1996) resulted from an attempt to structure early mathematical experiences in a paced progression towards the kind of mathematical skills expected of children when they begin primary school.

Whilst the intention of the Numeracy Strategy is for it to be inclusive, teachers will still face the challenge of providing the underpinning work needed by some as well as stretching those children whose mathematical knowledge has moved on.

ETHOS OF ACHIEVEMENT

Boyd and O'Neill (1999) describe the strategy employed by a Scottish local education authority to break the link between disadvantage and achievement. This included staff development on what makes children effective learners and setting out to encourage an 'ethos of achievement'. This will be characterized by what Brighouse and Woods (1999) describe as a 'proper recognition of a broad spectrum of achievement' and will involve a school-wide celebration of the progress of every child, not just the achievements of the most able. They suggest a number of ways in which this can be done, including the head teacher using assemblies to draw attention to personal achievement. They describe schools that have established a positive and purposeful approach, often in areas of social disadvantage.

The kind of school improvement activities they report create a fertile environment for an inclusive approach. Teachers have the confidence and opportunity to develop their own professional skills and part of this will be drawing upon the experience of colleagues in other schools. The divergence of mathematics teaching into 'main-stream' and 'special' can be reversed and a convergent 'mathematics for all' be fostered.

From this positive stance we move on to a study of school and classroom practices that spring from such an ethos.

TALKING POINT

How do you celebrate the achievements of the lower-attaining children in your school?

Part Two
Inclusive primary mathematics

5

Inclusion in primary mathematics

The majority of children identified as having special needs require
not specialist teaching but good, high quality and effective teaching.

(Aubrey, 1993)

MISSION STATEMENT

Inclusive mathematics teaching should be a seamless whole,
incorporating the principles and practices that enable every child to
be engaged in the lesson. The first section of this book has identified
some of the factors that have led to separateness. This section is
concerned with achieving convergence between the different
approaches described in the last chapter. The challenges are
considerable but they are not insurmountable, as will be seen in the
examples from schools.

INCLUSIVE PRACTICE

It is hard to draw a line and say when current practice becomes
inclusive practice. Accepting that inclusion is not a fixed point but a
process, it would be more accurate to say that what follow are no
more than developments that have evolved, to a large extent, from
the practice described in the first part of this book.

What might distinguish them is the intent to include all pupils.
Much of what is described has been done for a number of years and
the people concerned may be hard-pressed to recall exactly when they
adopted what might now be termed 'inclusive practices'. That makes
them no less valid than practices that have been introduced
deliberately at a defined point in time. Practice builds on previous
practice by adopting or rejecting it or, more often, by adapting it. It is
unrealistic, as Fullan (1996) has pointed out, to impose new practices
without sound preparation and then expect them to have the desired
effect. Any innovation requires people who are well informed and
confident in their ability if it is to be implemented successfully. A
more effective approach is to identify people who are already working
in the desired way and look to their experience and enthusiasm to

build up a momentum for change. Brighouse and Woods (1999) talk of *energy creators*, those enthusiasts who make things happen and inspire others.

This section draws upon the endeavours of such people and will demonstrate some of the approaches currently being used in schools that appear to be leading towards an increasingly inclusive approach. There will inevitably be occasions when schools need to give particular attention to individual pupils in ways that might not conform to a strict definition of inclusion. Some of the examples quoted are from special schools, which by their very existence breach many people's definition of inclusion. They are included because the experience of teachers in those schools is valid in that they are attempting to involve their pupils in mainstream projects and initiatives. Many are actively pursuing ways of making their mathematics teaching inclusive in one or both of two ways; firstly by including their pupils in mainstream initiatives and secondly by providing joint teaching sessions with mainstream primary schools. Whilst the pupils may be based in a segregated setting there is no doubt that the special schools concerned have a positive view towards providing inclusive experiences and many recognize that they are participating in a process that might well lead to their redundancy as separate institutions (Thomas *et al.*, 1998).

They have taken steps towards supporting mainstream schools, either formally or informally, in developing inclusive practices. In The Netherlands special schools are part of local consortia set up under the country's Weer Samen Naar School (Together to School Again) project. This nationwide initiative is intended to reduce the number of pupils in segregated special education, which in some parts of The Netherlands had risen to 5 per cent (Meijer, 1998).

The initiative mentioned above has been based on a structural change to the education system. To be successful there must be a corresponding change in the commitment of schools to keep those pupils who they might previously have referred for special schools. The reasons for referral might have been that the teachers felt unable to meet the children's needs within their classrooms. To change that perception is more than just a statement of principle, it requires a considerable shift in attitudes. This in turn depends upon teachers being confident that they now have skills and resources that they did not have previously and that they will receive ready and effective support during the difficulties they will undoubtedly face.

In countries where alternative placements were not so commonly available, such as Italy, there was a greater willingness to regard every pupil as being rightly placed in the mainstream class (Meijer, 1998). Even so, it is clear from personal conversations with Italian teachers that they need more resources if they are to give adequate attention to the pupils needing additional support. In Denmark such support is available for those deemed to need regular individual support, but there is a general feeling amongst teachers in a number of countries that the least fortunate are those who are struggling but do not meet the criteria to be designated SEN. These issues will be considered in more depth in Part Three but it is worth noting that, in the examples given, the schools have been able to allocate additional staffing to the classes. This is normal practice in special schools in the UK and Denmark but not always in other countries. Mainstream primary schools in the UK will achieve this through gaining additional funding either through their delegated funding for SEN or through being part of an initiative such as, in recent years, the Numeracy Project.

INCLUDING ALL CHILDREN

We now move on to considering whether mathematics teaching is being carried out in a way that involves every child. The situations described are usually the traditional one teacher to a class but in many instances there are additional adults. The roles of these adults will be clarified in the course of describing the classroom activities.

By allocating additional staff to support mathematics as well as literacy a school is indicating that it puts a strong emphasis on these core subjects. The support might be aimed at improving the attainment of the majority or, alternatively, targeted at the lowest-attaining pupils. It is important to be clear as to whether the additional help is targeted at improving the results of those who will affect the school's position in performance league tables or at raising the achievement of everyone.

There is debate about whether teaching can be done more effectively when the school is organized in ability groupings. Unstreamed or mixed-ability classes have been the norm in British primary schools but the demands of the National Curriculum have led to some schools setting for English and mathematics.

AN INCLUSIVE CURRICULUM

The development of an inclusive curriculum can be addressed through adaptations to:

- the format of the lesson
- the arrangements for group work
- the teacher's style of delivery
- the learning goals

- the materials used in the classroom
- the tasks presented to children. (Thomas *et al.*, 1998)

These aspects will be related to the mathematics curriculum and draw upon examples from the UK National Numeracy Strategy (DfEE, 1999).

Lesson format

The Numeracy Strategy decrees that every class is to receive a 45-minute mathematics lesson each day as a minimum. This is to ensure that all children receive a certain amount of mathematics teaching, which cannot be guaranteed if mathematics is taught within cross-curricular topics. Lessons are expected to follow a specified format consisting of an introductory part to the whole class, group work for the central part of the lesson and a final whole-class plenary session. This pattern is based on the Hungarian approach and is followed in primary schools in many European countries.

Whilst there is a clear logic to this approach if we consider the role of mathematics as a separate area of study in its own right, it could lead to mathematical skills being compartmentalized. It cannot be assumed that all children will work out the linkages between what is learned in the mathematics lesson and what skills to draw upon to solve a problem in an activity that is not considered mathematical. Children who have difficulty in transferring learning from one context to another, and that is a common feature for children with SEN, could be disadvantaged by too rigid a demarcation between 'mathematics' and other parts of the curriculum. There are sound pedagogical reasons for developing mathematical skills within broadly based topics and this principle should not be lightly surrendered. British primary school children's relatively high competence in problem-solving should not be sacrificed in a effort to raise number-crunching skills.

In an inclusive school, teachers will have identified the mathematical skills required in other areas of the curriculum. They will have developed strategies for creating explicit linkages between the learning of those skills and their application, practice and reinforcement in children's general learning experiences. They will be aware of the possibility of mental calculation activities resulting in parrot-fashion responses that are not supported by real understanding. In working with the whole class to 'rehearse, sharpen and develop mental and oral skills' they will include low-attaining children by asking them questions that bring to the front of their minds what they already know that is going to be relevant in the subsequent group work activities. This acts as what Ausubel (1968) would call an 'advance organizer', prompting the child by setting out the nature of the task and reminding him/her of the knowledge he/she already possesses that is appropriate to that task. Leading children towards the solution is not the same as 'giving them the answer'. Teachers will know this, but support staff will need to be trained to frame their questions in a way that draws this distinction.

Introductory whole-class session

During the first part of the lesson the teacher will be reviewing with the children what they already know as a preparation for introducing new learning in the central part of the lesson. The teacher should give every child the opportunity to make a positive statement about what he/she has achieved. This will be done in a way that demonstrates that everyone's achievements are valued and the whole class should be encouraged to share in the success of the lowest as well as the highest attainers.

The teacher will be faced with a wide range of competence in mental arithmetic. From the children's point of view this must not be seen as an ordeal involving public recognition of failure. They must be confident that they are not going to be shown up because they are not as competent as the higher achievers. They have to be made to feel secure that their personal achievement is accepted by their peers as being a step on the path towards achieving a common learning goal.

The challenge for the whole class is to recognize that every child is moving from one step to a further one. There is an undoubted motivational affect of competition between students but unequal competition can be demotivating. The teacher has to manage it in such a way that the contribution of the least confident child is encouraged and valued.

The low attainers should not be allowed to become discouraged because they are not keeping up with the majority, who should not in turn be allowed to relax because they are further ahead. Equally, the highest achievers should not be allowed to rest on their laurels, as can happen when a class contains a wide spread of ability with only one or two high achievers. Children who have experienced being the most able in a small primary school have a great shock when they come up against strong competition in a secondary school and this can set them back for a time. Many can and do adjust to the new pace and are motivated to work harder, but it is vital that they are supported through the process of coming to terms with the increased pressure. The child with a previously positive self-image can bounce back, but one who is not so fortunate is in danger of becoming disengaged. In extreme cases, schools can create special needs where none existed before. More frequently, they can exacerbate weaknesses in personal skills so that they become a hurdle to successful learning.

The same holds true of children coming from a special school into a primary school and a great deal of preparation is needed if they are to transfer successfully. It is in the whole-class session that their shortcomings are most readily exposed and the teacher has to strike a delicate balance between raising expectations and maintaining self-esteem.

A history of low achievement may have resulted in a child receiving additional support which in the whole-class session might be given by the support assistant in the form of low-key prompts, encouragement to 'have a go' or interpreting the teacher's words for children with hearing problems or additional language needs. Children with visual problems will need to have those compensated for in a lesson that relies on visual stimuli and those children with learning difficulties may need the teacher's words restated in words that are more comprehensible to them. It must be made clear to the others in the class that the purpose of this support is to help the children concerned participate in the interactive nature of the lesson.

When the class is, for example, chanting numbers, the learning support assistant can ensure that particular children participate by quietly anticipating the next number or giving them a visual clue. Interactive number games can be done in a way that enables all to participate by having several levels of involvement. Some children could be asked to say the next number in a sequence, while others can be asked to count on or back by a specified number. The teacher might also write the numbers on a blackboard, or ask children to write on the blackboard.

In this first session the teacher will be attempting to maintain a brisk pace to keep children interested and will have briefed the learning support assistant on what will be expected of the children and the levels of support that should be given to particular members of the class. To retain their interest the same concept may be presented in different ways. The more able children will probably make the linkages themselves and the teacher will use their responses to make the concept more explicit to the others. Words will have to be chosen carefully and all children should be familiar with those that are used frequently. Some, particularly children with autistic-spectrum disorders, will respond better to closed questions and need help with open questions.

Classroom routines should be established so that when questions are targeted at particular children the others allow time for a response and do not call out the answer. The learning support assistant may need to be alert to an unforthcoming child or help an uncertain one to frame a verbal response.

Discreetly supporting a child can involve more than prompting. It might mean observing the child's reactions, helping him or her to verbalize his or her thoughts, using apparatus to explain a concept or asking questions to draw out a response. It will also mean ensuring that the child conforms to the classroom regime and does not move around unnecessarily.

To maintain the pace of the lesson the teacher may have to curtail a topic whilst some children are still working towards being able to respond. The teacher can indicate to the learning support assistant how the task could be followed up or completed in the group work session. Ideally, this should be foreseen and planned for, but if this was not possible it may be preferable to plan with the assistant for the topic to be covered in group work on another day.

Group work

This session should be planned to teach skills and establish confidence. When a teacher or learning support assistant is providing additional support this session should be conducted with a recognition of the steps each child has made towards the learning goal. The new topic will have been framed in the context of previous work and children will be reminded of what they have learned previously. Appropriate vocabulary will be used and this might also need to be supplemented with vocabulary that most children will have grasped in earlier years. This vocabulary can be practised at other times of the day. Spatial words, for example, can be taught in physical education lessons and playground games are a good opportunity for reinforcing numbers, measures and directional words.

Those children receiving regular individual support will have learning goals that take account of the targets in their individual education plans. These may be mathematical targets or they may be connected with personal study skills. The Framework for Numeracy recommends that there should be no more than three levels of differentiation in group work. This may be difficult to achieve with groups with a range of individual learning needs who, in order to achieve a learning goal, will require a personal level of differentiation.

Teaching and learning styles

Within the class there will be a variety of preferred learning styles as well as the range of attainment and ability. Read (1998) asserts that inclusive practice should not be restricted to grouping according to ability but should take account of individual learning styles. He describes how some people are verbalizers but others learn through images; and developing this further it is possible to discern that particular subjects are taught in ways that favour one or other of these learning styles. The various strands of the mathematics curriculum have the scope to involve both styles. Whilst a particular style might have proved effective with the majority of children, teachers should be prepared to employ alternative strategies for individuals.

Clausen-May (1999) describes how mathematics education relies heavily on the spoken and written word even though it has scope for those whose strengths lie in their spatial skills. An emphasis on oral work and mental calculation will make it harder for those children to participate. She recommends giving children a concrete, visual model of the processes and describes how this could be done by using a Slavonic abacus.

Plenary session

The purpose of the final session is to bring the whole class together so that the teacher can review with them what they have learned. Part of the group work may have been to prepare a presentation and this session is an opportunity for children to report on what they have done.

The lower-attaining children may be learning something that others have already covered and this gives an opportunity for the whole class to reinforce their knowledge. The teacher might ask the assistant working with a group with lower-attaining pupils to lead the report back from that group, and the assistant will then involve the children at certain points in the feedback.

The teacher can then explain how the work described relates to the work of the other groups and fits into a pattern of concept development. The group's work will be given validity by being used to solve problems that have relevance for the whole class. For instance, work on money could be linked to the school tuck shop or to a forthcoming visit.

In this session the progress of individuals can be related to their personal targets, where it is appropriate to share them with the whole class.

Learning goals

The Numeracy Strategy (DfEE, 1999) expects schools to operate planning at three levels; long-term, medium-term and short-term. Long-term refers to the aims and topics set for a year, medium-term refers to what you will teach each term and when it will be taught; and short-term plans are the detailed weekly or fortnightly teaching plans for a series of five or ten lessons.

The range of ability present in an inclusive class will necessitate not only class targets but also group and individual learning goals. Some will be mathematical, others will be related to various aspects of children's personal development. For example, an individual education plan (IEP) might contain items concerned with attention or concentration, with presentation of work or with conforming to the pattern of behaviour expected in the class. Mathematical goals set for the majority will have to be broken down into smaller steps so that the progress of lower-attaining pupils can be planned for and recorded.

Where teachers have support from other colleagues in the classroom it is important that they too know what is planned and the part they will play in the lesson.

Parents will have been made aware of exercises the children will be expected to do at home. This may be at parents' meetings or through packs that the children take home.

Classroom materials

The teacher will need access to a wide range of materials. These might be stored in the classroom or, particularly if it is expensive and not used regularly, in a central resource. Some materials that are appropriate for the child's stage of cognitive development may be ones used normally with younger children. Structural apparatus is an example of something that will enable children to model processes until they have the mental schema to perform the operations independently.

Written or printed materials will need to be clear and not overload the child with information or demand a reading level beyond that which the child has achieved.

Having recognized the need to provide additional support materials for learning that are based on those used with younger children, it is important that they are presented in an age-appropriate format and do not appear too immature.

Tasks presented to children

The tasks should be related to the main topic but the level of difficulty and the amount of support for smaller groups or even individuals should be decided upon beforehand. We will look later at some of the practical resources available for teachers and preparation will include setting tasks at different levels with that equipment. Wherever possible the tasks should appear similar to those set for the rest of the class. Differentiation can be built in by providing a progression of activities within a task or by recognizing a range of outcomes from the task.

High-energy classrooms

An inclusive curriculum would be driven by teaching and learning processes that, in Hatch's (1999) words, support all learners equally and enable all individuals to reach their maximum potential. She talks in terms of a 'high-energy classroom', exemplified by four factors:

- Pace
- Know-how
- Investigating, Conjecturing and Proving; and
- Struggle.

Pace is maintaining a sense of expectation rather than moving through the curriculum at a high speed. Brighouse and Woods (1999) describe a teacher who ended every lesson on a cliffhanger, so that the children left one lesson anticipating the next. *Know-how* stresses understanding rather than memorizing routines. *Investigating, Conjecturing and Proving* should be integrated into mathematics lessons, not set for homework or done as separate projects to satisfy the requirements of an assessment. *Struggle* is there to remind us that there has to be a challenge if achievement is to improve. Breaking down learning into accessible steps is necessary when working with children with learning difficulties but there is a danger that it denies children a vision of the whole picture.

Learning is not easy and we cannot assume that by teaching mathematics in logical, digestible chunks the child will learn where that particular skill fits into the overall pattern or be able to retrieve it towards solving a complex problem.

Assessment

Children are tested for two main reasons: to compare them with other children and to find out why they are having difficulties. The assessment materials used in schools will serve one of these purposes but, whatever may be claimed by the originators, will not serve both. The distinction between the two purposes of assessment is not always clear-cut and this creates confusion when reporting to parents on their child's progress.

Firstly, summative assessment is a measure of attainment made at a certain time. It may be with a published assessment schedule that will give a score through which the child's attainment can be judged against those of other children. This will confirm that a child is a low attainer.

There are summative assessment instruments that give scores for the various strands of mathematics. To get a more detailed picture of the areas of weakness a diagnostic test is used. The results of this assessment are often represented as a profile showing the areas of relative strength and weakness.

Formative assessment is ongoing and many schools have devised their own recording systems. This will form a cumulative record that can be the basis of a termly or annual summative assessment by the teacher.

Assessment, of whatever type, is of most value when it informs teaching. It is the constant series of judgements that teachers are making about how children are learning. Unfortunately, in Brown's opinion (1998), the imposition of standard local or national assessment has been seen as the most important type of assessment and the professional role of the teacher has been undermined. He believes that the record-keeping required by politicians and administrators should be seen as secondary to the formative assessment carried out by teachers as a core element of their professional role.

He believes that the mathematics coordinator has a crucial part to play in the development of the ability of his/her colleagues to make well-informed assessments of their children's work and suggests that schools might begin by listing the purposes of assessment and comparing these with their current practice. In the context of inclusive mathematics, we would expect to see that a school was using methods of assessment that were sensitive to the wide range of attainment in the school. It would have the means of identifying where the child was having difficulties and these would be carried out within the classroom routine rather than necessitate withdrawing the child for a testing session.

PRINCIPLES INTO PRACTICE

In Chapter 1 we set out principles for an inclusive mathematics curriculum (see p. 20). We will now consider the practical implications of establishing those principles in a primary school.

Experience a broad and rich mathematical education

Children taken out of class for one-to-one teaching on an area of weakness as identified in their individual education plan are missing out on what the class is doing. Even when they remain in class they might be set tasks that again concentrate on areas of weakness and do not enable them to experience the richness of the subject. For example, they might be working on number bonds when the rest of the class is investigating number patterns. Instead of working separately on repetitive worksheets the work on number bonds could be presented as a task within the number pattern investigation.

When such a strategy is used it must be remembered that participation does not just happen. The involvement of every child cannot be left to chance, because children with difficulties have learned a number of avoidance strategies so that they are not put on the spot. The teacher will need to plan questions and work with the whole class on means of involving them. Marvin (1998) believes that this should go beyond questions that require children to recall facts and should give them opportunities to explain, explore and reflect. She suggests Circle Time (Mosley, 1993) as one way of encouraging children with learning difficulties to take part in discussions.

Be expected to do better than their perceived best

Expectations can be self-fulfilling. It would be foolish to advocate unreasonably high expectations but it can be damaging to set expectations too low. The balance is achieved by knowing the pupils and by setting tasks that they will find personally challenging.

Participate in projects and initiatives aimed at improving the teaching and learning of mathematics

In Chapter 9 we will consider some of the ways in which children with SEN have participated in projects and initiatives designed initially for mainstream education. We need to remind ourselves of the distinction Beveridge (1998) made between working together and working alongside and ensure that participation is meaningful, not a token gesture.

Benefit from a flexible approach

We have seen how teachers need to take account of children's individual learning characteristics and teach to them. This means recognizing that children are not necessarily better or worse at learning but that some learn differently. Teachers will have the capability to respond to the various styles and will have incorporated their knowledge of individual children into their planning.

There is ample evidence from school inspections that it is by improving the quality of teaching that there is a consequent improvement in the quality of learning. It is not the only factor, but few would dispute that it is a key one.

Have their achievements celebrated

A school that values every child will find ways of ensuring that each one experiences success and will have found ways of sharing that success with the whole school community. This could be through noticeboard displays, certificates presented in class or at assemblies and through personal records of achievement.

Benefit from their teachers having the confidence to identify their own strengths and weaknesses in teaching mathematics

The personal competence of teachers in mathematics varies considerably. Those for whom it is a strength are a school resource that should be used to support those less confident in the subject. As well as the kind of professional development discussed in Chapter 11 there are many informal opportunities for teachers and learning support assistants to learn from colleagues. A school climate where 'no one is afraid to ask', both staff and pupils, is one where difference can be accepted in a non-judgemental way and where help is given readily.

Experience a dynamic, not restricted, approach to teaching

The classroom environment will be, in Hatch's (1999) terms, in a high-energy state. This will apply to every child and the situation where those receiving additional or individual support are working with an assistant on the margins of the classroom will not exist.

Experience mathematics as an international language and use it as an effective means of communication with people beyond the school

As schools increasingly become involved in projects with schools in other countries the opportunities for enriching the mathematics curriculum are growing. Evidence of the participation of special schools suggests that there is scope for all children to be meaningfully engaged in such projects (EADSNE, 1997).

Benefit from an active commitment within the school and beyond that everyone is entitled to enjoy success in mathematics

Whatever might be stated in school policies it cannot be assumed that such a commitment exists in the day-to-day dealings of members of the school community. It has to made explicit and it must be reflected in a positive view of the subject throughout the school.

To many people the terms 'enjoyment' and 'mathematics' are contradictory. Higginson (1999) describes projects in Vancouver, Canada, which contradict this belief. These mathematical projects had strong artistic links and involved musical composition, the art based on geometric patterns and video animation. He notes the strong mathematical insights shown by primary-aged pupils that arose naturally from this work.

TALKING POINTS

What have we done to make our mathematics teaching more inclusive?
How can our children derive mathematical learning from creative activities?

6

Inclusive practices in primary schools

a child with learning difficulties
should not have the additional burden of low expectations
(comment overheard at a conference)

MATHEMATICS FOR ALL

The mathematics curriculum in schools should encompass the needs and learning characteristics of all children. Having recognized that as a basic principle of what has been referred to as 'inclusive mathematics', we will now consider how this can be achieved.

Responsibility for the implementation of a school's mathematics curriculum rests with the mathematics coordinator, whose role is analysed in detail by Brown (1998). He found that their work included: planning the whole-school mathematics curriculum; translating that plan into practice; monitoring its implementation; attending training courses and meetings; providing training for colleagues in school; reviewing and evaluating teachers' assessment of children's attainment; and teaching classes themselves.

Mathematics coordinators will generally feel competent to advise and support colleagues in teaching with the normal range of attainment but will feel less confident about children with SEN. For them to be successfully included in the mathematics curriculum, however, the coordinator will need to draw upon the expertise of the special educational needs coordinator (SENCO) who can provide detailed knowledge of the learning characteristics of those children who need additional and regular individual support. The SENCO will also be able to give advice to colleagues on methods of differentiating their teaching to accommodate the ways in which individual children learn most effectively.

Though the two coordinators may relate well on a personal level there are tensions between their respective roles. The mathematics coordinator will be expected to ensure that achievement in mathematics is raised across the school and will be concerned with maximizing the skills of colleagues and the resources available in order to improve the levels attained by the majority of children. The SENCO will be concerned that children who fall outside the expected norms will have their individual needs met. This could mean that class teachers are receiving two different messages. On the one hand, they will be encouraged to use approaches that have been found effective with the majority of children, but those same approaches, and whole-class teaching is a good example, can lead to some children being marginalized. The mathematics coordinator will be exhorting colleagues to maintain a brisk and lively pace to their lessons, the SENCO will be asking them to consider pacing their teaching so that the low attainers can keep up with the others. More able children will grasp ideas quickly, others will take longer, and the teacher will be concerned that by regularly revisiting topics the former will become bored.

Teachers will have a general idea of what is involved in differentiating their lesson delivery and will aim at keeping all children involved in lessons through setting tasks at different levels or by accepting a range of outcomes from the same task. They are unlikely, however, when teaching a whole class to be able to respond with the subtle nuances employed by teachers working in small groups or in individual teaching situations.

Schools are told that research shows that whole-class teaching is the most effective, while research by Harlen and Malcolm (1997) suggested that within-class ability grouping had a stronger effect on the progress of children of all abilities. At the academic research level such matters can be debated, but when teachers are pushed towards a particular teaching style on the basis of an outside body's inter-pretation of the research and what they can gain from courses and journal articles, then the scene is set for confusion and disagreement. It is not difficult to find research justification in support of didactic, interactive or any other style of teaching.

The challenge is to have an armoury of teaching strategies available upon which to draw when faced with a child whose progress in learning, or indeed attitude to learning, is outside the pattern with which the teacher is familiar. This occurs when the relationship between the mathematics coordinator and the SENCO is a productive one. Colleagues will appreciate that whilst their responsibilities may appear different their roles are complementary.

The studies that follow are taken from primary schools and are included to illustrate particular points relevant to the processes being promoted. At the end of the chapter we will consider the issues of planning, classroom management, developing teaching methods, promoting inclusive teaching strategies and differentiation in relation to practice in primary schools. We will consider the use of resources, including classroom support. In conclusion, we will try to identify how lessons in primary schools can match up to the model of the 'high-energy classroom'.

INFANT SCHOOL

The first lesson began with the teacher working with the whole class. They counted in chorus to 52 and she reminded them that on the previous day they had counted to 24. She involved J, a girl with specific language difficulties, by asking her 'what day is it today?' and then 'what day was it yesterday?'

She then led some mental agility work by asking them to count back and count forward. The questions were targeted at individual children and they were given time to answer. The class conformed to the rule that children be given 'thinking time' before they were prompted.

They did finger counting and then discussed how they could move beyond '10'. They then counted in 10s in chorus and then counted back in 2s.

After considering place value by discussing the meaning of 113, the teacher led an 'I say – you say' activity. She told them today's number was 10 and then said a number less than 10. They had to give the other number that would make a total of 10. When they gave an answer she asked them how they did it. Answers included 'I did it in my head', 'Seven fingers up, so there were three down' and 'I just knew it'.

They then brainstormed the different ways of expressing the 10, 7, 3 relationship and she wrote them on the board.

$7 + 3 = 10$, $3 + 7 = 10$, $10 - 3 = 7$, $10 = 3 + 7$, $3 = 10 - 7$, $7 = 10 - 3$, $7 + 3 = 3 + 7$.

Next was the 'Secret Number Game' where they had to write a secret number down and the other children could ask questions about that number. They were allowed 20 questions to get the answer.

Throughout this lesson all children were participating as a result of the teacher's skill in involving every one with appropriately pitched questions. When they had a difficulty they were guided towards the solution with suitable prompts from the teacher as part of the normal flow of the lesson.

The key principles being followed by the teacher were for the children to verbalize their ideas, and to use mental arithmetic. The conversation was lively and purposeful, what could be described as 'mathematical chatter'! During the whole-class plenary session the teacher used differentiated questions as a means of involving all the children. This lesson took place in the summer term and it was clear that the teacher had established a method of working that was understood and accepted by the children.

MATHEMATICS POLICY

All schools in Britain are expected to have written curriculum policies and the task of writing the mathematics one would probably fall to the coordinator. Brown (1998) suggests a format of what he believes should be a document developed through collaboration with colleagues. He suggests that it should include a section on the arrangements made for identifying, monitoring and supporting children with special educational needs. Whilst this would also appear in the SEN policy, one would expect a school committed to inclusion to see the writing of this document as the launch pad for a continuous process of curriculum development rather than as a one-off exercise to meet statutory requirements. It is conceivable that a school might decide that an inclusive thread ran through the whole document and might see that section as no more than a reiteration of what would be obvious to anyone who had read the policy and taken part in the work of the school.

SEN POLICY

Another infant school gives clear guidance on teaching numeracy in its Special Educational Needs policy.

- Encourage the correct formation of numerals at all times
- Encourage pride in the appearance of a page of work
- Provide as much practical experience as possible, and always try to explain new concepts in concrete terms, rather than in the abstract
- Discuss symbols such as $+$, $\times$, $-$, $=$, before pupils begin an exercise so that they are confident about what they have to do
- Encourage them to voice what they are doing. This will help them to work in the correct sequence
- Provide a ruler or number line to help with counting on or counting back
- Be aware that the pupil may be able to do things one day and not another.

The school's general guidelines for teachers state that:

> learning is far more likely to occur in a secure and stimulating environment in which the child feels accepted, despite his/her difficulties; relaxed and motivated. There is a variety of ways in which a teacher can help to create such an environment and incorporating them into his/her general teaching practice will not require particular expertise or make unreasonable demands upon his/her time.

They suggest the teacher should:

- Make sure that the pupil can see your face when you give classroom instructions
- Make sure worksheets are clear and well produced
- Begin each teaching session with some revision
- Set realistic standards
- Provide visual aids, which will consolidate information, stimulate interest and act as a ready reference
- Judge the pupil's ability on responses other than those which are written
- Discuss any difficulties together with the child
- Allow him/her to feel able to ask questions without fear of ridicule or judgement
- Give praise and encouragement. They are integral parts of the teaching/learning process
- Be patient; the child with specific learning difficulties may be forgetful and disorganized

and to remember that:

- The standard of work will be inconsistent from day to day
- These children have to work twice as hard to get half the distance
- It is vital that the child's knowledge be built on firm foundations
- Structured teaching using a multi-sensory approach is the most successful
- New concepts need to be carefully explained and be presented in a variety of ways
- The child with specific learning difficulties learns very little 'by the way'. Everything needs to be taught
- Constant over-learning is essential at every stage
- The child may put a lot of effort into a piece of work, but it may be well below the standard you expect
- The child may panic and be unable to organize his/her thoughts when presented with new work or faced with a stressful situation
- A coloured overlay may be helpful to a child who cannot handle black print on a white background.

IMPLEMENTING INCLUSIVE MATHEMATICS

The following points are drawn from observations made in British and Dutch schools.

Planning

Daily teaching is planned so that the child's individual learning targets can be followed within the general class teaching plan wherever possible. Additional support, rehearsing and reinforcement activities are planned in advance and reviewed after the lesson.

The teaching team, namely the teacher and any other adults working in the class, assess and review the work of the class each half-term, bringing together the information they have gathered to judge whether key learning objectives are consolidated. These key objectives are practised in a way that involves and benefits all the children in the class.

Any identified misconceptions or weaknesses are tackled at the earliest possible opportunity so that they do not impede the child's progress. There is a culture within the classroom where children are not afraid to ask or say that they do not understand without fear of blame or ridicule. This provides an open atmosphere in which differences in individual learning styles and pace are accepted.

Classroom management

Children are seated in positions where they can receive discreet help. Children with hearing impairments and their supporting adults are placed in a position where the teacher can ensure they participate in the lesson and receive the help they need.

Teaching methods

Teachers use a range of practical, verbal and visual strategies; they recognize that some children need more repetition and reinforcement than others. They vary pitch and pace to maintain interest and ensure that the attention of every child is engaged.

Inclusive teaching strategies

Teachers have planned questions specifically for particular children. It is suggested in the introduction to Framework for Numeracy that for children with hearing impairments and those for whom English is an additional language new vocabulary should be introduced and rehearsed. Schools also use this strategy with children who have learning difficulties.

The use of written instructions is minimized and flashcards, wall displays and other opportunities for visual presentation are used in relation to the lessons. They give visual clues to the target pupils and draw the attention of the class in general to the content of mathematics lessons. Interactive wall displays, such as ones which invite children to make a written or practical response, are present and are used by the children.

Children who present unacceptable or concerning behaviour receive mentoring and there is recognition of the value of success in the curriculum as a means of alleviating or resolving their problems.

Differentiation

The majority of children work together through the year's programme and always participate in new work in the plenary session. Low-attaining pupils experience success and many of them improve their attainments to within the normal range of the class.

In oral work when counting round the class the teacher points to a particular child to say the next number. Children are encouraged to respect the thinking time of others and not interrupt. This is reminiscent of the effect that occurs when television news presenters are interviewing someone on a satellite link. There is always a short time lag before they respond and this can be used as a metaphor to establish that thinking time is part of the class routine. When the correct answer is given, the class repeats it using a whole sentence.

Children are sometimes given the opportunity to discuss questions in pairs before giving an agreed answer. When a low- and a high-attaining child are paired, the teacher guides the children towards the skills of supporting each other and uses strategies and working practices that prevent the quicker thinking child from dominating the activity. Most children do not have an innate ability to help without overwhelming the child being helped; parents and teachers take years to hone this skill; and techniques, such as those used in the Circle Time approach (Moseley, 1993), encourage a patient and supportive atmosphere.

Support

When the teacher has the support of additional adults they are well-briefed on the children they are working with and the tasks they are expected to perform. They have received as a minimum basic school-based training on their role and some have relevant qualifications.

Teaching and learning resources

The classroom is equipped with a range of materials that give children the opportunity to investigate problems and rehearse their skills. The range of materials reflects the needs of the pupils and is not restricted by pre-set notions of what the majority of children of that particular age should be using. Classroom-based computers have software that enables children to work singly and in pairs on practising and extending their skills.

There are games and puzzles with straightforward rules in which all children can take part. The participation of some requires peer or adult support but this does not disqualify them from the activity.

Another rich set of experiences exist in the child's home and parents play an important part in their children's mathematical education. Good home–school links are potentially a powerful force in raising achievement and motivation but the school realizes that they need to be handled sensitively. Parents who are used to receiving bad news about their children's lack of progress are helped to build a trusting and positive relationship with the school. Schools realize that some parents may have found their own schooldays a less than rewarding experience. They might feel psychologically or even physically discomforted at the thought of going back into a learning situation, however welcoming the school might make it.

Homework

Denvir (Denvir *et al.*, 1982) associates 'impoverished home background' with low attainment. Whilst it would be unjust to denigrate parents, we know that some children begin school having had a much richer set of experiences than others. Whatever their circumstances some parents, as Harris and Henkhuzens (1998) point out, feel anxious about their own abilities and need 'extra encouragement and support from teachers to become involved in their child's learning'. They may not appreciate how the everyday tasks of running a home can be used as opportunities for learning. A book written in support of a television series is one of many now available that contain a wealth of ideas on how parents can help their children with mathematics (Walsh, 1988). The important point of such publications and programmes is that they are about parents working with children, not leaving them to work through exercises or watch programmes on their own, and the interactive nature of the homework is stressed.

Merrtens (1991) reports on a homework project for primary schools that involved a number of local education authorities in England and Wales. The aim was to encourage parents to become active participants in their children's mathematical education. The children took home materials from school to work on with their family. Teachers followed this up by including the outcomes of the homework tasks into the curriculum. Through the project teachers were able to make strong links between the mathematics children were taught at school and the mathematics they used at home and in everyday life. Similarly, children could relate their schoolwork to the context of home and family. Teachers developed children's problem-solving abilities by incorporating practical tasks into classwork and the working partnership between home and school was strengthened.

One of the infant schools described above has taken its role in promoting numeracy a step further by involving the parents, not as helpers but as learners themselves. An adult basic skills grant has been used to set up lessons for parents so that they can develop their own mathematical competence and have a better understanding of the work being done by their children. The school provides 'take home packs' so that parents and children could practise their skills together. The school has now joined forces with a local college and parents who take part in the adult numeracy course have a route to accreditation for their achievements. In doing so the school has demonstrated a commitment to lifelong learning.

Such local initiatives may be small acorns but replicated widely they could have a significant impact on employability and the growth of the national skill base. This seems a much more positive step towards decreasing social as well as educational exclusion than any number of political speeches about 'cycles of deprivation'!

HIGH-ENERGY CLASSROOM

It is probably true to say that experienced observers will be aware as soon as they go through the door that they are entering a 'high-energy classroom'.

Pace

As the lesson develops it is clear that the teacher is moving into gear, pausing at times to check that those who might be struggling are still involved. A learning support assistant keeps a watchful, but not overpowering, eye on them and knows how and when to intervene. This happens because the teacher and the assistant have a shared knowledge of every individual in the class and of the purpose, content and style of the lesson. They will have prepared well and will find time for a debrief at a convenient time during the day.

The pace stretches the higher achievers without leaving out the slower learners. It is purposeful but not fast, and at intervals the teacher sets the former short exercises that they can do independently while he or she focuses on the latter.

The length of the whole class lesson is judged according to the known range of attention spans in the class. Even those with a short span are sufficiently motivated to remain interested.

Know-how

The children are used to the routines and follow them comfortably. Their desire to achieve their learning targets is such that disruptive behaviour does not normally arise and if it does is met with strong disapproval from the class. Where the modifying of such behaviour is an individual target the rest of the class will understand this and usually ignore it.

It is clear from their responses and their written work that the children are moving from memorizing towards understanding what they are doing. The staff recognize that for some this means a considerable amount of experience before the children have combined their skills into a meaningful approach to a task. Ample and varied practice is given so that the knowledge gained becomes established as a mental construct, or 'know-how'.

Even that stage is not taken for granted and teachers use opportunities in the mathematics lesson and in other activities to check whether the knowledge is securely fixed. They also alert learning support assistants to those opportunities and ensure that the resources are at hand for this kind of follow-up.

Some children may be closely observed, by means such as pupil tracking, so that teachers are aware of not only of what they are teaching but also what the children are experiencing within and beyond the classroom. Assessment procedures take account of both informal and formal assessment so that a full picture of the child's learning profile is built up. The child will be enabled to play an active part in assessment and through this process, which will be ongoing, priorities can be established and revised and resources allocated accordingly.

Teachers are confident that if their own 'know-how' is insufficient they can look to colleagues for support. This could be informally, from an appointed mentor-colleague or a visiting advisory teacher or from a school-based teacher support team (Creese *et al.*, 1997). These are made up of colleagues with particular expertise and are intended to provide support and assistance in dealing with learning and behavioural difficulties. Such a team established to support colleagues in developing inclusive mathematics might include the SENCO and the mathematics coordinator. It is part of the underlying principle of this approach that someone who had at one time sought help from such a team might develop his/her own skills to the extent that he/she could be an effective member of it. As the writers point out, many effective teachers modestly play down their own skills whereas to share good practice might be a sound base from which to begin influencing other colleagues.

Investigating, conjecturing and proving

The scene in the classroom is of a purposeful environment in which everyone understands what is expected of them and knows how and when to get help. They will not be passively receiving information but actively working on solutions to the tasks they have been set. Every child will be engaged, with no one left out. Whatever hurdles they may face, the teacher finds ways of giving them a role in a group task. Wrong answers are regarded as a positive step towards the solution, and no one is afraid to 'have a go'.

Children use their skills to investigate a wide range of problems and this is apparent across the whole curriculum.

Struggle

There is a sense of challenge that stimulates children to move forward. The steps of learning have been broken down to make them accessible for the low attainer, but in doing so the teacher has not lost sight of the goals being pursued. Opportunities are taken to enable the child to see where the current task is leading so that even the least able can feel a sense of anticipation. Athletes use the phrase 'no gain without pain'. That might seem an extremely harsh dictum to apply to the classroom but the suggestion that with a little mental exertion you might achieve more than you thought possible has its merits.

In the high-energy classroom the child with individual learning difficulties will not have the additional burden of low expectations.

TALKING POINT

How can you make yours into a high-energy classroom?

Including special schools

...special schools as an integral part of an increasingly inclusive system
(Wiltshire, 1998)

CURRICULUM INCLUSION

Much of the debate on inclusion has focused on *where* children are taught. Aubrey (1993) believes that this has masked another important question − *what* are they taught? Curriculum inclusion does not depend on where a child is taught but on whether the child is receiving an education that is set within the context of the curriculum available to all children. It is the means by which all children can participate in a common curriculum in a way that is, to repeat Dearing's phrase, wholly relevant and meaningful.

We might pause and consider the significance of this concept, which is by no means universal. It has blunted the sharpness of the divide between special and mainstream education, though, it must be said, it has not yet removed all the barriers. Whether it is a real achievement or a selective use of terminology is a local issue. Some special schools are fully on-board mainstream initiatives and their children regularly participate in activities that involve pupils across the whole spectrum of ability and needs. Others have a sceptical view of being involved in such initiatives and maintain a distinct separateness.

The following two studies are of special schools involved in the UK Numeracy Project.

SPECIAL SCHOOLS IN A MAINSTREAM PROJECT

Six special schools' mathematics coordinators and the head teachers received two days' training from the local numeracy team. During this course they drew up, with the help of the project team, an audit of their school's mathematics teaching and from that an action plan for their school.

The team also gave each school five days' consultancy support and during their visits they and the mathematics coordinators monitored the action plans. Schools had funding to release the mathematics co-ordinators from class teaching for five days so that they could spend time in other classes. Their involvement in colleagues' lessons was planned with them in advance and time was allocated for joint evaluation after the lesson.

One of the schools was a primary school for children with severe learning difficulties and the following lesson was observed during the first year of their involvement in the Numeracy Project.

The teacher followed the three-part lesson format. She began with a revision of previous work on the numerals 0 to 10.

The class joined in a taped song, supplied with the project materials, about ten bees flying around a hive. The numerals were on cards that were pegged to a line running across the front of the class. The teacher stopped the tape when a number was mentioned and asked a specific child to find that number. Some children needed support with this task, such as one child with poor motor control who was physically guided by a learning support assistant. A hyperactive child was prompted to keep on task but most of the others found the correct one without help.

The class was then divided into groups for different tasks. Some continued to work on numerals whilst others carried out sorting tasks. For the final plenary session they sang to the song *Ten Green Bottles* once more using the numerals.

A PRIMARY AND A SPECIAL SCHOOL IN PARTNERSHIP

The next case study takes curriculum inclusion a step further. The project began when the special school and primary school head teachers were both at a conference on inclusive education. They agreed that it would be worth seeing what the schools could learn from each other.

Each Tuesday six children from a school for pupils with severe learning difficulties join a local primary school for literacy and numeracy lessons. In the primary school's inspection, Teaching and Learning had been identified as an issue that needed attention in order to improve the relatively poor achievement by pupils in the school. The head teacher felt that, as over 20 per cent of the school's pupils were identified as having special educational needs, the staff might benefit from seeing some of the strategies used in special schools.

The special school had appointed one member of staff to co-ordinate inclusion opportunities and she had informal discussions with the primary school head teacher. Reciprocal staff visits were arranged which gave some of the primary teachers their first experience of a special school.

It was agreed that a group from the special school would come to spend one day a week in the primary school. A group of six 10- and 11-year-olds were selected as being the ones most likely to cope with and benefit from what was a new venture for everyone, staff and pupils alike. It was decided to place them with a class of 9-year-olds, who were briefed on disability before the first visit.

The project began as an exercise in social integration with the joint group doing 'getting to know you' activities and later exchanging letters at other times in the week.

A programme of visits and meetings involving staff, governors and parents ensured that they were all aware of the project and the commitment of all three groups was seen as essential.

It had been agreed initially that there would be half-termly planning meetings and at one of these it was decided that the project should have a curriculum focus. The primary school was taking part in the National Numeracy Project which was supported by a set of clear learning objectives. These seemed to offer a sound basis for planning joint teaching activities.

The content of each session was planned at weekly meetings involving the class teacher and learning support teacher from the primary school, the inclusion coordinator from the special school and learning support assistants from both schools.

The pattern of each lesson mirrored that recommended in the Framework for Numeracy (DfEE, 1999).

They begin with an introductory session aimed at involving all the pupils in which the class teacher ensured that all the children were involved by targeted questioning. However, on a number of occasions the combined class was divided into two groups. A group containing some of the special school pupils worked separately when it was felt the content of the whole-class session would not be meaningful. It was a long-term intention to work as a single whole-class group but that was seen as a stage of future development that would happen when the time was right.

The following observation is of a group containing five special school and two primary school pupils. One of the special school pupils would have normally been with the main group but, because of some behavioural problems, had stayed with the special school teacher on this occasion. The topic was shapes and the teacher had a collection in a cloth bag. The tasks included:

- taking a shape and matching it to a similar one on the table
- taking a shape and naming it

- identifying a shape by touch
- finding a particular shape by touch.

During the group work session the class teacher is responsible for the bulk of the class and works with them on place value. There are also three combined groups, which consist of two special school and four primary school pupils, led by the special school teacher, a learning support assistant from the primary school and a learning support assistant from the special school. Each group works on number work at an appropriate level.

The whole class comes back together for the final plenary session. This is led by either the primary school teacher or the special school teacher.

At the end of the day there is feedback to the class teacher on the work done in the combined groups and teaching objectives are set for the next week.

One of the primary school pupils, who had been in a combined group, made sufficient progress to be able to return to the main teaching group and his place was taken by another child who was weak at mathematics.

The special school has brought apparatus to support their children who have particular needs. In many cases commercially produced teaching materials are designed to give a visual impact but result in confusing some children. Written and diagrammatic material has been modified by, for example, using enlarged text and printing it on a distinct background. As well as making it more readily accessible to children with visual handicaps it has been helpful for other children who find it difficult to understand material presented in the usual way.

Other purpose-made resources have been produced and, whilst it is admittedly time-consuming, the exercise has given the primary school teachers an insight into the way in which materials can be differentiated.

The head teacher of the primary school regards one of the most important outcomes of the project to be the raised awareness amongst her colleagues. They have realized that there is a place in individual education plans for targets focusing on mathematics as the skills involved are utilized in other areas of the curriculum. They have developed a deeper understanding of strategies for differentiating the curriculum and it has helped them address in a more effective way the issue of involving children with a wide range of individual needs in the mathematics curriculum.

The involvement of learning support assistants has highlighted their crucial role in the teaching and learning process. On her visit to the partner school, her first to a special school, the primary head teacher noted the favourable adult-to-pupil ratio and realized the potential this gave for employing a range of teaching strategies for meeting a diverse range of needs. The freshness of such an observation, of something that has become taken for granted by staff in special schools, should prompt them to consider whether they are using support staff as effectively as they might.

A key lesson has been the value of openness. It is to be expected that however much goodwill is present all the interested parties, pupils, parents, governors and staff, will have their concerns and misgivings. These have been addressed when they arise, in some cases pre-empted by being raised at an early stage, so that they do not become barriers to the development of the project. The school's adviser, who also has a special needs brief within the local education authority, takes a close interest in the project.

All those involved recognize that pragmatism is an essential element of the relationship between the two school communities. Whilst the ideal might be full inclusion there are a number of reasons why it is advisable to delay that development.

PACING LEARNING

The notion of whole-class teaching can be modified. The example given is for one part of class to be with the teacher and the remaining group with the learning support assistant, if the class has one.

In an observation in a primary SLD school the session began and ended with the whole class together. Group work took place in as many groups as there were adults available.

Cooperative learning in heterogeneous groups is considered by Thomas *et al.* (1998) to be a desirable trend towards future inclusive practice. This would help to overcome the culture shock that children can experience when moving back into mainstream education from special schools.

It is recognized that progress through the learning targets set out in the Framework for Numeracy may be at a different pace and it may take two years to cover what is set out for one year. It may also be necessary to add small steps, and these could be based on the strategies described in Chapter 5.

One of the difficulties that arises when children work through such a framework at a slower pace is that they will in time be undertaking activities that have been designed with younger children in mind. The most obvious example of this is when 15- and 16-year-old students with severe learning difficulties are working on learning targets intended for 5-year-old children. It is vital to their self-esteem that the contexts for practical work and problem-solving should be appropriate for their age even if the level of mathematical skill is related to younger children. This can be most readily seen by looking at the illustrations in mathematics schemes for infants. These are often of objects familiar to that age group but that would appear childish to older students. It is more relevant and better for their self-esteem if they are given tasks related to the kind of practical applications that would occur in their overall learning programmes, such as putting them in a vocational context.

The routine of the daily maths lesson recommended in the framework should be built up over several weeks, and the teacher should aim firstly to establish daily oral and mental work.

It is recognized that children with severe and complex learning difficulties may need work that builds a foundation for the first levels of the framework. Again, they may take significantly longer to cover the targets set out for each year and it is probable that they will cover only the first few stages of the programme.

POINTS OF CONTACT

In the introduction to the Framework for Numeracy (DfEE, 1999, p. 24) it is claimed that the approach being promoted is applicable in special schools because it promotes:

- *Planning from clear teaching objectives*
  Clearly defined teaching goals are set out in the framework from which teachers in special education can select those which are most appropriate given the current stage pupils have reached in the development of mathematical knowledge. Whilst the progression is helpful to teachers, the ages at which those teaching goals become relevant will vary considerably.
- *An emphasis on oral work and mental calculation*
  This has led teachers to review their current approach, particularly where they have assumed that their children do not possess the skills to benefit from this kind of teaching. Work mentioned earlier on styles of learning might lead teachers to consider whether those struggling with written computation and recording might not achieve more with a verbal approach.
- *Visual interest*
  Attention and motivation can be maintained through the use of visual images to represent the mathematical processes being undertaken, as with the abacus.
- *Involvement and interaction*
  As we have already noted, participation has to be planned for. Teachers will need to ensure that all children in the class understand what is involved in working cooperatively and will

use directed questions and other strategies to engage the interest of those who might have difficulty in following the lesson.

- *Keeping pupils working together as far as possible*
For many the view of special education has been of a pupil following an individual programme, often in one-to-one teaching situations. There has been a belief that children with special needs do not possess the skills of sharing and cooperation that are necessary to make joint working feasible. Many children, and not only ones described as having special needs, will find this hard and all children will benefit from being taught the strategies of co-operation.

  This is more in line with the interactive approaches which see the pupil as an active modifier of information rather than as a passive recipient (Smith, 1990). In the early stages of developing a curriculum for children with severe learning difficulties in the 1970s much use was made of an objectives approach based on behavioural principles. The introduction of the National Curriculum led to a reappraisal of the curriculum that had become common in special schools for pupils with severe and profound learning difficulties.

- *Whole-class teaching*
In the joint special and primary school initiative the whole-class lesson had been modified into two large group lessons.

- *Taking longer to cover teaching programmes*
The length of time required by children with learning difficulties to cover the programmes is going to affect the extent to which they can participate readily in mainstream class lessons. Where the topic can be covered in multi-level tasks it will be possible but if the task requires specific skills not possessed by the low-attaining pupil then alternative grouping may be necessary. As teachers and assistants develop their planning and working practices such instances should decrease.

- *Extra small steps for children with mild, moderate and severe learning difficulties*
The extent to which learning targets are broken down into small steps will depend upon the learning characteristics of the children. The degree of precision and gradation needed for children with severe learning difficulties may not be necessary for those with mild or moderate learning difficulties. For the latter the normal learning targets might be appropriate with smaller steps available for when they meet particular problems. For children with profound difficulties the small steps will be defined in relation to learning targets aimed at the development of skills in the personal rather than the mathematical domain.

- *Building up routine over several weeks*
Children are comfortable with routine and this is particularly

beneficial for those with learning and behavioural difficulties. It helps children to maintain concentration and encourages them to complete tasks in time for the next part of the lesson.

- *Establishing daily oral and mental work*
  The introduction of mental and oral classwork is challenging for schools that have been used to relying on practical and written mathematics. Strategies to engage children's attention and encourage them to respond include stories with a mathematical theme, songs and videos.

- *Routines for main part of lesson and plenary*
  By having established routines children learn how to respond in an acceptable manner in each of these settings. Those who disrupt the pattern will experience peer disapproval which is often more effective than adult disapproval. This is particularly so when the majority of the class are motivated to achieve their learning targets.

- *Concentration on strong oral or communication technique that promotes interaction*
  Where children have difficulties in communication the support in the classroom should be focused on enabling them to participate. This will need patience and toleration from the rest of the class and the teacher should make a positive statement when someone shows this kind of consideration.

- *Good range of practical activities*
  Repetitive use of the same practical materials will lead to a decrease in interest and motivation, which in turn leads to boredom and disruption. A fresh practical activity that draws upon the skills the children already have can provide an impetus to involvement.

IMPACT ON THE SPECIAL SCHOOLS

Both subject specialists and special school teachers appreciate the benefits of working together. Specialists, who might previously have considered children with significant learning difficulties as being outside the normal range of expectations, gain an insight into the way special school teachers mediate the curriculum so that it becomes meaningful to those children.

For the special school teachers, the subject knowledge of the specialist extends their understanding of mathematics so that they can see the place of each activity in the process of learning mathematics.

The rigour and precision of the Framework for Numeracy ensures that no one can hide behind woolly statements or blanket generalizations. The emphasis is on what the child can do and what will be the next stage in his/her learning.

It defines the role of the mathematics coordinators and they are clearly expected to give leadership and support to colleagues. The coordinators have a definite role in planning all mathematics teaching in the school, not just their own class. They are expected to plan with the class teacher and in one of the schools they also ensured that learning support assistants had advance notice of what they would be doing each week.

Both schools found that they had to make adaptations to the framework and time allocation had to be extended. This presented difficulties for the special school working with the mainstream school in that the latter would be aiming to work through the framework within the set timescale. This difficulty could be overcome if the staff from both schools had time to plan for differentiation but without that it had been necessary to operate separate lessons.

The introduction of smaller steps of learning was beneficial to mainstream pupils who were not keeping pace with the rest of the class or needed attention paid to gaps or misconceptions in their mathematical knowledge. It made all three schools consider the extent to which children possessed the foundation skills on which mathematical knowledge is built.

PUPIL INVOLVEMENT

The key question is – *did the children participate in a meaningful way?* The answer from all the staff concerned would be resoundingly positive. In the first activity the majority of pupils were involved in saying the numbers, and this spread over into informal use of numbers. The term 'zero' generated considerable spontaneous verbalization and the teacher skilfully used this interest.

MUTUAL BENEFIT

As one head teacher said, 'inclusion can only work if the teachers have commitment to the principle, enthusiasm to overcome the hurdles and the professionalism to persevere.' The costs in terms of time and energy draw heavily on these precious commodities and it is reasonable to ask 'what are the benefits?'

Teachers and learning support assistants have found that colleagues from special schools are skilled in adapting materials to a greater extent than they might have thought possible. They also show that well-designed materials have the scope to be used with children across the ability spectrum. They are able to provide a bank of objectives for teachers to refer to when catering for a child who falls outside the norms for that class.

At a progress conference teachers described some of the ways they had adapted the framework to make it applicable in their schools. In advance of lessons they had looked at the activities set out in the framework, modified the objectives to take account of individual learning needs and prepared differentiated materials. Amongst the mainstream children who were seen to benefit most from the joint lessons with the special school were those who were not formally identified as SEN but were known to be struggling in mathematics.

TALKING POINT

Is there contact between primary and special schools in your area?

8

Mathematics beyond the classroom

An approach to the mathematics curriculum
which builds on the deep connections
the discipline has with all other forms of human activity . . .
will permit the development of a number of rich alternative curricula.

(Higginson, 1999)

THE OUTDOOR CLASSROOM

Making mathematics education meaningful to children means more than importing 'real-life' activities into the classroom. Aubrey (1999) reports on reforms in The Netherlands where mathematics is regarded as a human activity rather than as a subject.

This begs the question 'Why not take the classroom into the real world?' The environment provides a wealth of opportunities for gaining mathematical experiences by providing what Aubrey refers to as 'rich context situations'. She draws a distinction between the Dutch approach of drawing mathematical learning from the context and the British practice of deciding subject content and then attempting to make it relevant with concrete materials.

Immediately outside the school gates a wealth of mathematical features will present themselves to the careful observer. The shape, colour and size of houses, windows, doors, roofs, the numbers used on letter boxes, the numbering of lamp-posts, road signs, bus stops, petrol stations, shops; the list can be added to by introducing one or two of these features with each journey. Drawings can be made of objects with numbers on and these can be used on a display of different ways of using numbers. Photographs or video film are useful means of bringing the ways numbers are used to children's attention.

It is common for us to follow the same route regularly and, as a result of familiarity, not register what we see. This kind of exercise encourages children to observe and deliberately to note what they see. The information can be used later to recall the journey and putting the features in order is a good sequencing exercise.

Vocabulary can be practised and used in a realistic setting and contexts can be found for using number, spatial and sequential words.

The teacher should be selective and not expect every child to grasp everything. For the one or two children who have individual learning targets that vary from those of the majority in the class it may be better to focus with them on one or two concepts and use each new observation to draw out the concepts and vocabulary relevant to them. Take as an example the study of postboxes. Some children might have the task of answering questions based on the written information on the plate, others may be finding the times of collections from the box while some might be asked to note the colour and shape of the box, with perhaps a task related to identifying the numerals used.

Before moving on they would be asked to speculate on how far it is to the next postbox and whether the information gained will be the same. At the next postbox the tasks would be repeated and the information recorded. Some initial comparisons would be made and a full review of the findings made on return to the classroom.

Every child would have been involved in investigating, conjecturing and comparing and all would have something to contribute to the fund of information that had been gathered.

Bell's (1992) book is a rich source of ideas for gaining mathematical experiences in the local environment. He shows how, with planning and the cooperation of local shops and organizations, it is possible to set up activities that bring mathematics alive for the children. In some of the suggested activities it may be advisable to brief the host that there will be children working at different levels and that they may not all be carrying out the same task.

MATHS TRAILS

Teachers may not relish the prospect of taking a large class on to busy roads and a lot can be done within the school grounds. A nursery school set up a maths trail in the playground. Each station was numbered and the maths trail box contained activities to be done at each one.

The first stop was at the front door that had painted on it a large smiling face inside a circle. Other objects were painted on the adjoining walls and the question was 'What shapes can you see?' There were suggestions for questions that gave scope for every child to answer, such as 'Can you touch some writing?' (the words *Welcome to our school* were in large script at a child's eye height); 'What colour is the door?' and, to extend the activity, 'How many rectangles are in this door?'

At the climbing frame they practised spatial words and then they moved on to a mural of a clock and blackboards. The number words, the names of shapes, words like *shorter than, taller than, shortest* and *tallest* could all be brought out of this display. The trail continued with a model bus and train which took them to the last point, the sandpit, which represented the seaside in this inner-city location.

RESIDENTIAL EXPERIENCES

Birmingham, a large urban education authority in England, made it a matter of policy that all children had at least one residential experience during their time in primary school. It is a feature of such centres that programmes are developed in consultation with teachers and are related to the school curriculum. Mathematics can be studied from a new perspective when children look at plants, trees, hedgerows and paths.

The journey to the centre will probably involve travelling on main roads and motorways and these provide an example of numbers being used in a particular way. The road numbering system is in most countries a combination of numerals and letters – M5, A26 – and a motorway junction offers a wealth of source material for directional work and symbols.

Strict minibus driving regulations mean that journeys have to be carefully planned in terms of time and children can be involved in this exercise. Where the journey involves a sea crossing a number of other factors can be included, such as the relative speed of the minibus and the ferry.

Upon arrival at the residential centre certain routines have to be established and these involve concepts such as 'allowing enough time to carry out set tasks', 'being ready at a certain time' and 'having an appropriate number of people to carry out the tasks'; remembering that 'many hands make light work' but 'too many cooks spoil the broth'. In setting out the daily programme the group can identify a variety of ways in which mathematics can be applied and these can be stated as learning targets for the week. For example, a group from a special school on a camping week in Brittany discovered that they used mathematics when:

- They got up (time)
- Set out places for breakfast (number, one-to-one correspondence)
- Decided how much bread and milk to buy (proportion and ratio)
- Decided what money they needed to take to the village shops (unit value, estimation).

At the end of the day they reviewed the decisions they had made in the morning and decided whether they needed to revise the quantities they purchased for the next day. Some noted that by the time they got to the shop there was not much bread left, so the group on shopping duty would need to get up earlier. There were also complaints about the amount of milk, the number of spoons and cups. Most critically, no allowance had been made for the staff to have their essential cup of tea!

During this discussion the cost of familiar items was noted and, using conversions based on an approximate exchange rate, comparisons were made with the cost of those items back home.

PLANNING

The staff had been able to undertake a preparatory visit before the first group went (Robbins, 1993) and in subsequent years they found an increasing number of ways in which these visits could enrich the school curriculum (Robbins, 1995). Booklets were prepared using material from a number of sources, both commercial and school-produced, and were completed by each child as a personal record of their visit. The contents included sections on planning and saving for the visit; routes, times and distances; what would have to be bought during the visit; places to be visited; a daily diary; and a report on the visit.

CURRICULUM OPPORTUNITIES

Being away from busy streets and centrally heated or, in summer, overheated buildings leads to an enhanced perception of temperature and daylight. Whilst it is probably light before the children wake up, they can be reminded that in winter they may be starting out for school in semi-darkness and it may well be dark when they arrive home. The residential experience can be the starting point of a daylight recording project that will run through the following school year. The children can match their own observations to the official times of sunrise and sunset published in diaries and newspapers. Questions such as the meaning and purpose of 'lighting-up times' can be discussed. They could be set the task of finding the daylight hours on their birthday and make predictions on what the weather will be like. Would someone having a winter birthday have a different kind of party from a friend with a summer birthday?

This would bring in consideration of weather and the two most significant measures; temperature and rainfall. These could be introduced by asking what type of clothing would be suitable on each person's birthday.

A record could be kept of wet playtimes and at the end of the year this data could be analysed and presented in graphical form.

BRINGING THE CONTEXT INTO THE CLASSROOM

Within the school grounds there are sources of mathematical experience that can be exploited. Many schools have now established maths trails that involve the children interpreting clues in order to move on to the next point in the trail. The clue could involve recognizing a shape or a number, solving an arithmetic problem or completing a sequence. Children can be involved in setting up as well as solving the trails.

Trails set up indoors could include interactive tasks on notice-boards that lead the children to the next clue. School corridors are often seen as a means of getting from one place to another but they do have considerable potential as a source of educational experiences. One primary school that has three floors has used the high walls of the staircase to paint a mural of the universe. As you go up the first few steps you move through the earth's atmosphere, then you reach the moon and, a number of steps further on, the sun. By the time you reach the top floor you are in the Milky Way. The whole display gives children an idea of the relativities in the universe and objects, such as aeroplanes and space satellites, help them to appreciate the difference between travel within the earth's atmosphere and the exploration of outer space.

The school library is another rich source and two teachers decided to work together in drawing learning out of some of their children's favourite stories. The stories were built around spatial words, which are important as they underpin the development of mathematical concepts.

One of the most popular was of some naughty little bears getting *out* of bed, climbing *through* the window and *down* the tree, climbing *over* the wall, *under* the bridge, *around* the lake, *between* the rocks, *through* the woods and *up* the hill.

A teacher led one group in the task of preparing a course in the hall that would follow this storyline. Tremendous ingenuity and energy were expended in obtaining suitable objects and setting them out. When it was finished the other group came in with their teacher and at each obstacle the course builders instructed them, using a full sentence, such as 'go under the bridge'.

As they followed the instruction the children doing the task repeated the sentence. Then roles were reversed for another story, which was about a boy who imagined that his garden was booby-trapped. The teachers had also prepared flashcards, each with one of the key words, and the appropriate one was placed by each obstacle.

In a whole-class plenary children were asked to find specified words and to say the whole sentence containing that word. The next day the topic was revisited by setting tasks that involved sentence building with these words. Those who were able to write sentences did so, while others built sentences with cut out words or wrote the missing word on worksheets where the key word had been omitted from the sentence. The words were again practised in their next physical education lesson.

There is inevitably a degree of contrivance in following a 'rich-context' approach and Aubrey recognizes that the distinction drawn above is not always a clear-cut one. The important consideration is that the child develops the skills to move between mathematics the subject and the applications of mathematics. For children who are known to have difficulty in transferring knowledge, any experiences that build a bridge between their skills and the problem to be solved are going to be of value.

EARLY COUNTING

The origins of counting go far back into prehistory. Probably one of the earliest applications of one-to-one correspondence was by the Stone Age farmer when keeping count of his sheep. As each of his flock passed through the gate he would put a stone on the wall and if on their return there were more stones than sheep he knew that he was being bothered by a predator, either wolf or human. This application developed from the concrete to the representational when the farmer made marks on the wall to represent each animal. The origins of written calculation lie in these prehistoric tallies.

Whatever historical period is being studied there will be opportunities for counting and calculating, from Roman legions to ships in the great sea battles. The word 'centurion' derives from the number of soldiers under that officer's command and the core of the word can be related to other words that describe 100, such as 'century'.

'Cent', 'centime' and 'centimetre' refer to both a whole number and a decimal fraction, such as $2.49. Some children have difficulty in appreciating the dual meaning of this figure, particularly with amounts of less than ten in numerical form. They will need considerable practice, preferably with real coins, before they consistently write four francs five centimes as FF4.05 rather than FF4.5 or two pounds seven pence as £2.07.

Similar mistakes occur when recording measurements, with the added complication of distinguishing between centimetres and millimetres. The key to understanding this is place value, which may be used correctly when written calculations are presented in vertical form but not in the recording of practical investigations. The skill performed successfully in a structured task does not transfer readily to a less-structured presentation. Teachers should be aware that some children have greater difficulty than others in making this association and exercises involving the use of coins and measures in realistic situations are another way of building an understanding of the importance of the position of the numeral in relation to the decimal point.

MATHEMATICS IN THE ENVIRONMENT

The flower bed or herb garden may not be the first place one would think of looking for sources of mathematical activities and yet the growth of plants conforms to definite patterns. Again, as was noted earlier, people look but they do not always see. So many impressions never become conscious observations unless attention is drawn to them. A tree in the school grounds is a living example of the relationship between climate, soil and the influence of other forces. The leaves grow and die according to a pattern that all children can appreciate. Closer observation will reveal that the growth of smaller plants is affected by the presence of the tree. It is also influenced by other large objects, like hedges, roads or buildings. All these phenomena can be measured and expressed in terms that are meaningful to children. It may require the teacher to draw out the concepts from a number of examples before some children grasp the significance of what they observe but in doing so the learning of the whole class is being reinforced. There may even be a role for more able children in finding different examples of particular phenomena. Having to explain to others is an effective way of improving your own understanding and teachers can use the findings of more-able children as a source of experiences for the others.

The teacher could display an assortment of leaves or flowers for the class or group to look at. They might ask some of the class to describe one, without pointing at it or naming it, using words from a list of mathematical vocabulary. The task for the class is to decide which leaf is being described. This activity can be adapted to use with other objects, both natural and man-made, that might be collected on a walk. Some large, heavy or fixed objects do not lend themselves to being collected and the use of the video or still camera would make it possible to study them on return to school. For example, the designs of litter bins in a park give scope for work on shape and capacity and the design of them can be a link between mathematics and technology. Some pupils may be given the task of gathering factual information whilst others can be asked to investigate the reasons for particular designs and why certain materials are commonly used. This will involve gathering data and using that data imaginatively. This could lead on to consideration of the relevance or non-relevance of particular information.

Words related to Time that might arise in a 'mathematics in the environment' project include the four seasons and children can be asked to note the characteristics of spring, summer, autumn and winter in terms of the appearance and growth of natural objects. 'Faster' and 'slower', 'old' and 'new' are amongst the words that the National Numeracy Project would expect 8-year-olds to be able to use appropriately in a mathematical sense. Comparatives – 'long', 'short', 'fast', 'slow', 'wide' and 'narrow' – are used more readily by young children than the comparatives, 'longer', 'shorter' and so on. A plantation of young trees is a good example of differential growth and again extension tasks can include using data collected by the whole group to pose further questions for investigating. There will be reasons why trees planted at the same time have grown at different rates and factors such as proximity to tall trees or walls, a shaded or well-lit position and density of undergrowth can be conjectured upon and then measured and recorded. This would give the opportunity to reinforce positional words; such as 'in front', 'behind', 'next to', 'apart', 'middle', 'edge', that younger children would be expected to know and use correctly.

MEASURES

Children move from using non-standard measures to learning the conventions of metric measurement, be it metres for distance and height, grams for weight or litres for liquids. Terms such as tall and short, more and less, full and empty are translated into precise measures that are universally recognized and accepted. Once children have grasped this concept and can perform and communicate measures they are in possession of a very powerful tool. To some children this does not come readily and they first have to appreciate the significance of measurement as a means of communication. By setting tasks that involve going beyond the immediate location of the group, collecting information on distances or heights and reporting back, they will appreciate that the information has to be accurate and reliable. It must also be the correct information, not something else that they happened to see. Teachers will be familiar with children who become distracted and come back with irrelevant or ambiguous information. When the task is to gather information that is to be used by the rest of the class there is peer pressure to carry it out properly and greater motivation for the others to help them get it right, rather than to dismiss their efforts as meaningless.

BUILDING VOCABULARY

The environment provides a wealth of opportunities for using and developing the vocabulary of mathematics in a meaningful way. There are obviously limitations on the extent to which teachers can take children out of the classroom but a well-planned day or residential educational visit will play an important part in bringing alive what they have learned, or perhaps half-learned, in the classroom.

EVALUATING EDUCATIONAL VISITS

Visits can be evaluated either by the staff who participated or in a group session involving the children. One school devised a format that covered all aspects of the visit. The version used for the session with the children included a recall of each day, what they had recorded in their daily diary and what they thought they had learned. Prompts were given, ranging from ones related to personal development, such as 'what did you learn about being with others?', to ones related to the curriculum, such as 'what mathematics did you learn?'

The staff evaluation included items on the personal and social benefits for individual children, the curriculum gains, the effectiveness of the planning, the feedback from the children and from their parents.

In the present context, the identification of the mathematical opportunities that arose in the visit, which will be many more than envisaged beforehand, form the basis for setting curriculum goals for future visits. As with any such activity it is hard to quantify the gains for each child that are due solely to a particular activity but gains in observational skills and facility with mathematical skills will, almost certainly, result in improved achievement.

TALKING POINTS

What mathematics could be learned during your next educational visit?
How will you provide experiences that every child will find meaningful?

9

Mathematics through partnership

embedded in potentially-rich learning situations that are
interesting and relevant for students and
enable all to participate and grow.

(Higginson, 1999)

WORKING WITH PARENTS

The partnership between school and home is the single most
significant relationship in supporting a child's learning. The
importance of pre-school learning is now widely accepted as is the
recognition that the lack of mentally stimulating interaction between
parents and children can prove a disadvantage when the child begins
school. It is often the case that the parents themselves have poor
numeracy skills. For them, as Bynner and Parsons (1997) point out,
their limitations in mathematics reduce their prospects of employment.
As the people with poor numeracy skills come, predominantly, from
poor households, a pattern of considerable disadvantage emerges and
suggests a link with children whose attainment is low and with those
identified as having mild or moderate learning difficulties. Any
measures that can improve the skills of these parents will improve
their life opportunities, create a more educationally enriching home
environment for young children and go some way to preventing
children needing special educational provision later in their school
career.

One infant school set out to improve the numeracy skills of parents
whose children attended the school's Family Centre for children aged
3–5 years. This was part of a Family Numeracy project involving 14
local education authorities (LEAs) aimed at helping parents to
'improve their own literacy, help their children with numeracy and
give an immediate boost to children at risk of failing in numeracy'. All
the projects involved schools in areas of disadvantage that had below
average attainment in mathematics in the national assessments carried
out at 7 and 11 years of age.

There were sessions for parents to work on their own numeracy
skills with the help of adult education tutors. In other sessions parents
and children worked together on the ways that early numeracy
learning could be developed in the home.

The outcomes were encouraging. Both parents and children made considerable progress and the children who took part made far greater gains than their peers who were not on the programme (Basic Skills Agency, 1998).

There was no set pattern as to how the local education authorities worked within the programme; a diversity of approaches was encouraged and the evaluation of the project, carried out by the National Foundation for Educational Research (NFER), identified characteristics of effective practice. They were:

- A minimum of a weekly one-hour session for parents and their children and at least two hours each week of tuition for parents alone.
- A minimum of two 45-minute sessions each week for the children for up to ten weeks.
- A firmly structured numeracy curriculum.
- Focus on progress in a selected and achievable range of numeracy skills and concepts.
- Meaningful and explicit links between the different strands of mathematics.
- Accreditation for parents that recognized their achievements.

The teaching strategies considered most effective have much in common with those promoted by the Numeracy Project and it is clear that the Family Numeracy Programme is consistent with that initiative.

One of the goals of the Family Numeracy Programme was to form a bridge between school and 'real world' maths for children most at risk of underattainment in mathematics (Basic Skills Agency, 1998). We will now consider others ways of bridging this gap.

PARTNERSHIPS

Despite a political climate where schools were put in competition with each other there are many examples of schools working together. Arnold (1995) reports on several projects that involved schools, local education authorities and universities cooperating in school improvement initiatives.

A number of special schools gained experience of belonging to a mainstream partnership as a result of the UK's Technical and Vocational Education Initiative (Harland, 1987). For one all-age special school for children with moderate learning difficulties the experience of being in a TVEI partnership with nine secondary schools and a college of further education encouraged the development of working relationships with neighbouring primary schools. Even before this, many special schools had established links with neighbouring mainstream schools (Jowett *et al.*, 1988), but the later kind of partnership moved the process from being concerned predominantly with the movement of pupils into the arena of professional, curricular and school development.

The special school applied the TVEI partnership model in establishing a formal grouping with 12 local primary schools. They undertook a number of joint staff development activities, including meetings for SENCOs and workshop sessions for learning support assistants.

NUMBER CONCERT

Having decided to focus on mathematics partnership the mathematics coordinators from the schools met to plan a series of school-based activities and a joint event that would all take place in a particular week. The culmination of Maths Week was a concert held in the local church, the only building large enough to accommodate all the children involved. Classes learned a common set of songs with a mathematical theme and presented them at the concert. As everyone had learned them it was very much a participative event and the children from the special school played a full part in the proceedings.

> Five little teddy bears jumping on the bed,
> One fell off and bumped his head.
> Mother phoned the doctor and the doctor said,
> No more teddy bears jumping on the bed.
> Four little teddy bears . . .

Other songs were: *Six little ducks*; *The ants go marching*; *This old man, he played one, he played nick nack on his thumb*; *The animals went in two by two*; *Number rhumba*; *Disco tables* (the multiplication tables sung to a disco beat); a *Number rap*; *Rock around the clock*; and finishing with a song written by some of the children, entitled *The five days of Maths Week*.

BUSINESS PARTNERSHIPS

As primary schools have become involved in education and business partnerships, opportunities have become available to them that were previously restricted to secondary schools. One partnership has organized a practical mathematics day entitled 'Maths at Work' at which companies set real problems for the children from primary schools. Children from a special school took part in this event.

'Design a drive' was set by a company that specializes in roads, drives and paths. The children were set this task:

> A customer has a drive of x metres long by x metres wide. The customer wants it paved with slabs, either square or rectangular, and would like the costings of each in plain and coloured slabs. There is a labour charge of £x per 10 slabs laid. There is a discount of 10 per cent on every ten slabs laid. What additional information do you need?

As well as preparing working drawings, an extension task was set of preparing a scaled-down version of the designs to show the customer.

The children decided what they needed to know and asked the company for the information. They then worked out the costings for the different ways of laying the drive.

A transport company set a task on its drivers' delivery schedules. The children looked at a three-day schedule and were asked questions such as: 'which branch takes the earliest delivery?' and 'what is the latest delivery time?' They were also provided with a map and asked to mark in the driver's route.

This kind of activity shows children the relevance of the mathematics they learn in school and there was clear evidence of a high level of motivation throughout the day.

A primary school that was involved in an international project asked the lorry drivers to send cards from the different European countries they delivered to.

Another primary school had visiting musicians from the city's symphony orchestra and they too agreed to send postcards from each destination of their forthcoming international concert tour.

This kind of project generates real data that can be used both in mathematics and geography. A range of tasks can be set so that there are some within the capabilities of the lower-attaining children. Careful planning will ensure that they are able to make a genuine contribution, not a token one, to the overall data collection and its subsequent presentation. Some children will be asked to present it graphically, others pictorially, verbally or even in a dramatic or musical performance. Rather than the more able doing the interesting work while the less able struggle through uninspiring worksheets, it could be the latter who are given the opportunity to explore mathematics in a creative way. Schools who have been involved in business partnerships have found that they can bring a degree of enrichment to the curriculum for all children that cannot be achieved through simulated 'real-life' projects.

INTERNATIONAL PARTNERSHIPS

Mention was made in the last chapter of a special school's visits to France. The school's international partnerships began when it linked with a similar school in Birmingham's twin city in Germany. Frankfurt has a commitment that all its school pupils have at least one week during their school career at a residential centre, Wegscheide, which is in a mountainous area near to the border that divided the country until 1989. This was the venue for a joint residential trip.

Prior to the visit a joint in-service training course was held. During the course time was devoted to planning the residential, which has since been followed up by reciprocal visits to England and Wales. Another session looked at ways in which the schools could learn from each other in mathematics education. Fortuitously a German publisher had published a translated version of the worksheets that accompany the Mathsteps materials (Robbins, 1991b). This opened up the possibility of children experiencing some basic German vocabulary, and the meanings of words could be readily found by referring to the English version of the worksheets.

SOCRATES

The international dimension was extended by the school's co-ordination of a European curriculum project with similar schools in Germany, Denmark, The Netherlands and Northern Ireland. The project involved a class in each school recording what they had eaten during a specified week. The schools exchanged this information together with the results of further investigations into where the food was bought and its cost in the local currency. This was compiled into a booklet that each school was able to use.

This partnership has continued support from the European Union's Socrates programme. Many schools have taken advantage of the opportunities to develop international links. These have developed into partnerships with schools in several countries working together on joint projects funded through the Comenius chapter of the European Union's Socrates programme. There has been concern that many of these links were at the level of a professional exchange of information (EADSNE, 1997) and did not lead to active participation by children at a curriculum level, which was a feature of the example given above and of more recent projects involving special schools.

Those that have belonged to partnerships have found them rewarding. Pupils have enjoyed exchanging information through letters, videos and books as well as by telephone and fax. The task of preparing a fax calls upon writing skills and sending it requires a knowledge of numerals and sequencing numbers. Time differences between countries need to be taken into account and this can lead to interesting discussions on what people in other countries might be doing at that moment.

Mention was made in the last chapter of a daylight measuring project. This task can be extended through international partnerships by introducing data from partner schools of daylight hours in their countries. Schools in Finland and Estonia would be able to describe phenomena like 'white nights' and the midnight sun in a direct and real way that would be far more meaningful than if presented in a textbook.

AUTONOMY OR TEAMWORK?

Teachers have an established tradition of classroom autonomy (Lacey and Ranson, 1994). External forces, such as school inspections, have 'opened the door'. The kind of partnership activities described above serve as a means of enriching the curriculum and create a new spirit of openness and teamwork.

There are teachers who expect to be able to meet children's needs alone. When that is no longer possible they have traditionally looked to someone else to give that child an alternative curriculum. Inclusion brings a new set of expectations and with them the realization that active participation in mainstream education is only achievable if the teacher is able to share the workload with another adult in the classroom. The next chapter deals with the effective management of classroom support, which at its best qualifies for the description 'teamwork'. As Lacey and Ranson point out, collaboration is not merely the act of working together in the classroom, it is to do with a 'belief that the problem can only be solved by combining the skills, knowledge, understanding and experience of all those involved'.

TALKING POINTS

How do you include parents in their children's mathematical education?
What opportunities does the school have for working in partnership with other schools or businesses?

Part Three
Supporting an inclusive approach

10

Support in the classroom

Teacher support is a key factor in
the integration of pupils with special needs
in mainstream education.

(EADSNE, 1999)

TYPES OF CLASSROOM SUPPORT

The report, quoted above, on provision in 17 European countries, describes the additional support that is made available to teachers when they have a child with special educational needs in their class. There is a general recognition that some children's needs present challenges that are beyond the experience of many teachers. Even when they do have an understanding of what is required, the pressures of teaching the whole class may prevent them from giving adequate attention to individual children.

Many countries operate a system where a specialist teacher, such as one trained in the education of deaf children, will work in the classroom alongside the class teacher on a full or part-time basis. These may be permanently attached to the school or be part of a central team managed by the local authority. External support in some countries comes from visiting teachers from special schools.

Other professionals, such as speech and language therapists, visit schools regularly and are permanent members of staff in some special schools, particularly those for children with physical disabilities.

Whereas in the past these professionals would have taken children out of the class to give them their specialized treatment, there is a growing trend towards them working in the classroom. Through joint planning with teachers they will incorporate their specialized work into the curriculum of the school. So the physiotherapist helping to improve a child's movement will be contributing the development of spatial skills and this will be recognized as a contribution to the mathematics curriculum.

Teachers and speech therapists will agree on developing the understanding and reproduction of words within the mathematics vocabulary and the tasks of learning support teachers have broadened from teaching reading to helping the teacher to differentiate teaching strategies and resources across the whole curriculum.

As well as support from specialist teachers and from other professions, schools in some countries have employed learning support assistants. Originally they were assigned to give intensive support to one child but they are now expected to be available to many more children, in some cases to the whole class.

ROLE OF SUPPORT STAFF

'The role of support staff is to help you make sure that each child plays a full part in every lesson' (DfEE, 1999). Jerwood (1999) notes that in some schools assistants are not used effectively and could be considered a 'wasted resource'. He believes that the key to effective support depends upon the clarification of the assistant's role and the teacher's skills in managing other adults in the classroom. Often there is a lack of understanding on the assistant's part about what is being taught and on the teacher's part about the purpose of classroom support. In some cases assistants will be expected to devote their time fully to an individual child.

Learning support assistants can be frustrated by the unwillingness of teachers to utilize their talents and abilities. There have been misgivings about whether an assistant is 'helping' or 'teaching'. Teachers' associations have expressed concern at the possibility of the work of qualified teachers being done by less-qualified staff on lower salaries. This has created an unfortunate atmosphere in which assistants feel in some cases exploited, in other cases underused. In a survey of the professional development available to learning support assistants, Dew-Hughes and her colleagues (Dew-Hughes *et al.*, 1998) found considerable confusion amongst the assistants about their role.

This confusion is shared by teachers as well as by the children who do not always know how to relate to an assistant. A lot will depend upon the way the teacher relates to the assistant as the children will quickly pick up clues as to whether the assistant should be treated with the same respect as the teacher.

Many felt inadequately prepared for their work and would have welcomed a formal qualification. At present there is a range of accredited courses but the successful completion of a course does not always lead to an increase in salary. Whilst this is an important issue the main concern in the present context is the definition of the roles and responsibilities of a learning support assistant in mathematics lessons.

Ensuring participation

It is interesting to note that the advice to the teacher in the Framework for Numeracy sets an inclusive note by emphasizing the assistant's role in enabling the child's participation in the work of the class rather than an exclusive focus on his or her special needs. Too often classroom support has meant the helper doing tasks that the children should have been encouraged to do for themselves and it requires skill and awareness to enable but not to take over. The purpose of the role is to make it possible for the child to work alongside others and to participate as fully as possible, not for the assistant to be an intermediary for the child.

There are situations when the assistant has to represent the child, such as interpreting and reporting the movements and expressions of a non-verbal child, but the emphasis should be on the child communicating, as far as possible, on his/her own behalf.

A learning support assistant working alongside a child with impaired hearing should know in advance the vocabulary to be used in a lesson and will have rehearsed it beforehand with the child. The child will then have some clues as to the content of the lesson should he or she not grasp everything that the teacher has said. On realizing this the assistant can give the child a brief prompt rather than have to explain so that the child misses what the teacher says next.

An assistant with a child who exhibits emotional or behavioural problems will recognize the limits of the child's attention span and will be alert to the signs of impending boredom and disruption. Before the lesson the assistant and the class teacher will have agreed on what steps to take when this arises. Again, the purpose of any intervention should be to bring the child back into active participation with the rest of the class as soon as possible. This might involve having resources available to realign the activity so that child retains interest and, by quiet prompting, to keep the child on task.

In order to carry out their role effectively learning support assistants will need to develop the skills of observing children; monitoring their response to tasks set by the teacher; giving the teacher accurate feedback on the child's performance; being ready to intervene and being able to time their intervention so that it is not too soon to prevent independent achievement, but not so late that the child has become disengaged from the lesson.

The assistant needs to be alert to what for the child might be critical points in the lesson and be ready with a means of explaining what the rest of the class may have grasped in terms that the child can understand. Assistants must remember the importance of the child relating to the other children in the class and not allow the child–assistant relationship to be so strong that it excludes the teacher and the rest of the class. There is a danger that by giving certain children their sole attention learning support assistants actually reinforce that child's differences in the minds of the other children.

They have a role in preventing undesirable occurrences, or

situations that could lead to an extreme reaction, by being able to focus on particular children more directly than can the class teacher. A child's wrong answer could spark off a reaction, either from themselves or from the rest of the class, so whole-class sessions will have to be handled tactfully by both teacher and assistant working together. They should be giving the same messages to the class and avoid giving the impression that they are applying differing standards or expectations. This is particularly difficult when the teacher is dealing with the whole class and the assistant has to employ a particular behaviour management strategy with an individual child that appears at odds with what the teacher has said. It is vital that they have discussed this fully beforehand so that they can explain what they are doing and why they are doing it in consistent terms that will be understood and appreciated by the rest of the class.

The class might be presented with a task that should be within the individual child's capabilities but some might not understand what the teacher requires or see the link between the task and those skills they already have. In this instance the learning support assistant has to act as mediator between task and child, either by repeating the teacher's requirements or prompting them into recollecting another occasion when similar skills were used. They will say things like:

> 'Let's go over what the teacher has just said.'
> 'Do you remember when the class was asked to solve a problem about . . .?'
> 'Can you remember how we found the answer?'
> 'What did we do first?'
> 'What did that tell us?'
> 'What did we do next?'

There is a subtle distinction between prompting and giving the answer and learning support assistants should have the opportunities in training sessions to develop the art of questioning and practice using different types of questions; closed ('what number is between three and five'), open ('tell me what you have discovered about the number pattern?') and leading ('have you thought of putting this shape over here?').

Individual education plans

Learning support assistants have a key role in relating targets on children's individual education plans (IEPs) to the learning targets of the mathematics curriculum. The teacher will have indicated how the IEP targets can be related to the forthcoming mathematics lesson and after the lesson will review progress towards them with the assistant.

Children who are aware of their own areas of weakness may themselves have negotiated the targets in the IEP and requested extra help with something they are finding difficult. This might involve tracking back from what the child is finding difficult to previous learning that underpins the skills and knowledge needed in the current task. The Mathsteps materials (Robbins, 1996) originated from a desire to set out developmentally based strategies that could be used by learning support assistants.

Group planning

There may be several children in a class, particularly those needing additional support, who would benefit from common approaches and it might be appropriate to draw up a Group Education Plan. The assistant's role would be to work on mathematics-related targets from that plan and to report back to the teacher on the progress made by each child. This would not be through a formal assessment but from observing and talking with the children.

Individual programme

Those needing regular individual support may do better if they are following an individual programme in the second part of the numeracy lesson, after participating in the whole-class session. They may need apparatus to support their thinking. This will be more effective if the teacher has planned this aspect with the learning support assistant so that there is a mutual understanding of the purpose and parameters of the support.

Professional support

In supporting the children the learning support assistant in turn needs support from colleagues. The SENCO will play a major part in identifying those children who need support and in allocating the time of a learning support assistant. The role of the mathematics coordinator is to recognize which teachers and classes need an additional adult for certain aspects of the mathematics curriculum. Either, or both of them, will have resources that can be used to give a range of differentiation to lessons and to be used with groups or individual children.

Reappraisal of the role

Inclusion, according to Florian (1998), requires a reconceptualization of teaching roles and responsibilities and a reappraisal of the role of support staff. Thomas *et al.* (1998) recommend that learning support assistants should be encouraged to work flexibly and that their role be seen as being an educational one, not a caring one. They should work in the classroom and withdrawal of pupils from the classroom should be kept to a minimum.

It is essential that there is good communication between members of the classroom team and that the SENCO and mathematics co-ordinators plan together with class teachers and, whenever possible, the learning support assistants. Similarly, class teachers must have the opportunity to plan and review with their in-class support staff.

Professional development

Thomas *et al.* (1998) report the comments of learning support assistants who felt that their training focused on the functional aspects of their role and did not give opportunities to develop a broader understanding. They make the point that teachers as well as learning support assistants have a wider set of training needs and that professional development should go beyond curricular knowledge into the 'ethos behind inclusion and the organisational practice that makes inclusion a reality'.

It should develop their ability to respond to the diversity of needs in the class rather than be concerned with supporting one child. This is a very different style of working which requires adjustment on the part of both the teacher and the assistant. Ideally, they should receive training together so that they can explore the implications of working in this way and agree to a set of ground rules.

The topics covered in training should include the various methods of differentiating the curriculum so that assistants can appreciate the rationale for following a modified approach or using alternative materials with some children. An understanding of the distinction between teaching and learning would help them to appreciate that one is not necessarily a consequence of the other and that what the child sees and hears may not be what the teacher intended. A basic understanding of the learning process can be developed into a more detailed knowledge of the ways in which that process can be delayed or distorted. As the assistant will be spending a lot of time in close contact with children, there will be many times when the child makes a statement that, to the trained ear, reveals a misunderstanding on his or her part. To be able to recognize that and to have sufficient knowledge of the subject to be able to correct the misconception immediately is likely to be more productive than leaving it until the teacher can give the child individual attention. There will, of course, be times when the assistant realizes that the situation should be referred to the class teacher. Both courses of action require confidence and openness between the two colleagues and where this is established the children benefit considerably.

They will need to be able to communicate relevant information to colleagues and this means being able to filter out the relevant from the irrelevant. Time is a precious commodity and the opportunities for discussing the children's responses and judging progress must be used purposefully and efficiently. This does not mean a formal structure to meetings but it does involve an acceptance from the teacher and support staff, and from other colleagues in the school, that daily review sessions are important, should be done properly and should be free from interruption.

SUPPORT FROM OTHER SOURCES

One of the features of the Numeracy Project is the establishment of local teams of advisory teachers who act as project consultants and spend a considerable amount of their time in the participating schools. They need time with coordinators and should to be able to observe, or even participate in, maths lessons. They can negotiate with the mathematics coordinator how their time should be used to best effect in the school. It is often a combination of giving in-class support, of training teachers and of supporting the mathematics coordinator. They have access to a bank of materials at their central base and can loan these to schools, who might decide to buy their own copies.

AWARENESS OF TEACHING STRATEGIES

The amount of knowledge and insight needed to be able to support a teacher in the classroom is considerable. When the role centred on caring for the needs of the individual child, good maternal skills were a sound basis for performing it adequately. As the role has developed into one which plays a key part in enabling all children to participate in the school curriculum, an understanding of the basic principles of teaching is essential. This is not to say that all assistants should undergo an equivalent training to teachers. They should, however, be given the chance to acquire sufficient knowledge for them to be able to appreciate what the teacher is trying to achieve. They should be able to recognize the different strategies being used by the teacher with individual children. They should understand why the learning environment is organized in the way it is and they should be able to undertake work with children in accordance with the teacher's requests.

All schools work differently, however much the country's education system demands conformity. New members of staff will soon find out if they do something that is contrary to the school's established culture. For this reason many schools prefer to undertake the training of learning support assistants themselves. It is common in special schools for assistants to receive training from the teachers as part of the school's in-house professional development programme. Schools have set up joint training arrangements with local colleges and universities so that there is a blend of the theoretical and the practical.

Whilst this has many strengths, there is also value in meeting colleagues from other schools. As Dew-Hughes and her colleagues (1998) found, assistants would welcome training in the teaching of literacy and numeracy as well as in, what for many was a high priority, handling emotional and behavioural difficulties.

The handbook for classroom assistants (Aplin, 1998) that accompanies the Framework for Numeracy has a number of practical teaching scenarios with pointers on how learning can be fostered in those situations. In a series of school contexts – *mathematical games and activities, the home corner, in the playground* – there are prompts for the assistant that guides them into ways of utilizing them. There are suggestions of *Questions to ask* and *Things to notice* that focus the work of assistants and give them a conceptual framework within which they can report back to teachers on their work with individuals or groups of children.

There should also be opportunities to develop their own study skills as well as tackle any weakness they might have in literacy or numeracy. Many of them have a different life experience from teachers and this can bring a richness and empathy to the classroom that a teacher alone cannot. Learning support assistants can be much more than an 'extra pair of hands'; they are a valuable, and in some ways, unique educational resource.

TALKING POINT

How are learning support staff in your school involved in planning and reviewing lessons?

Staff development

It ain't what you got,
it's what you do with what you got.

(Mae West)

HUMAN RESOURCE

Every manager of every organization has at some time or another thought how much better it would be with a change in staff, and schools are no different. Head teachers believe, sometimes rightly, that a new teacher would make the world of difference to an underachieving class. School governors and local authorities might in turn feel that a new head teacher would raise the standards of an underperforming school.

Whilst there may be some justification for concern the solution is based more on hope than hard evidence. An injection of fresh talent and enthusiasm into a school can be extremely stimulating but it does depend upon the selection procedure finding someone who is actually more effective than the previous incumbent, and this is not always certain.

The reality is that most school leaders have to work with the staff that they have. New head teachers often inherit a staff that does not have the balance of age, skills and interests that they would be looking for had they been appointing an entirely new staff. It is therefore essential that they establish the aptitudes and abilities of the current members of staff and engage in a process of staff development towards what is needed by a school in the new century.

This can be achieved through a self-review process such as that described by Brighouse and Woods (1999). They suggest a process of 'appreciative enquiry' which would ask in terms of the school's mathematics education:

- what are the good aspects of our teaching?
- what could it be like if we had more of the good aspects?
- what do we want it to be like?
- what will it be like?

The final question sets a target for staff development and will give the process a sense of direction. The process will identify strengths and shortcomings and will build a shared commitment towards improvement.

The school's most expensive resource, accounting for over 80 per cent of its running costs, is the human one. It is also the most flexible resource and the one most conducive to change.

COPING WITH CHANGE

The pace of educational change has quickened in all countries in the past few years and shows no sign of slackening. If change is to lead to improved teaching then all those working in schools need to spend some time acclimatizing to new circumstances. Many of the changes in practice described previously depend upon teachers learning new skills or refreshing old ones. They need training to prepare them for new approaches and ongoing professional development as they work through the implementation of those practices in the classroom (Thomas *et al.*, 1998). All teachers need to have a broad knowledge of the mathematics curriculum and know how to modify materials and approaches (Aubrey, 1993). Read (1998) argues that teachers need a greater understanding of the different styles of learning if they are to teach effectively. Whole-class teaching is not the same as the traditional one-way approach of the teacher transmitting information to rows of dormant children. It is not a return to telling but requires instructing and explaining through a dialogue with the child (Merrtens, 1997). At its best it is a lively, interactive approach that brings every child into active participation.

One-to-one teaching calls upon a different set of skills and it can be demanding for both the child and the teacher. Group work gives the opportunity for closer observation of individual children's responses to the task and enables the teacher or assistant to intervene more readily. It is again a much more intensive style of teaching that involves constant adaptations to the content and pace of the session.

According to Boyd and O'Neill (1999), our knowledge of how the brain functions has grown significantly in recent years and they describe how research findings were communicated to teachers so that they could adapt their teaching strategies accordingly. A working group had been set up to consider evidence on how the brain works and had recognized the importance of a 'balanced diet' of learning approaches. The group was concerned that current preoccupations with assessment were leading to a concentration on a narrow range of cognitive attainment and were not recognizing the many facets of intelligence (Gardner, 1993).

Good morale and high expectations are features of schools where the staff have shared values and maintain a consistency to their overall approach. This arises not by accident but as a result of good management and an ongoing process of discussion and curriculum development.

Learning support assistants have much to contribute to this process and staff development programmes should be planned with their participation in mind. As with interactive teaching, effective professional development builds upon the strengths of the school and we need to move away from the idea of 'staff receiving training' to one of 'staff participating in their own development'.

PERSONAL PROFESSIONAL DEVELOPMENT

Effective learning is built on what is already known. This is true for adults as well as children. Before requesting further training teachers should be sure of what they already know, what they need and why they need it. One school established peer-mentoring arrangements for staff, developed from the mentoring approach it had adopted for supporting newly qualified teachers (NPC, 1994). This was separate from appraisal and is usually carried out with a trusted and respected colleague. The following set of questions form part of a process of self-review that highlights areas in which the teacher feels the need for further training and helps to prioritize those needs.

Personal Professional Development − a self-review

Assessment and record keeping
How well did I assess my children and their needs at the beginning of the year?
How did I use the information from the previous teacher?
Did I get any surprises?
Did anything go wrong because I had under or overestimated what the children could do?
What have I learned from this experience?
Are the records I keep useful to me and to others?
What are my main professional development needs in the area of assessment and record keeping?

Planning
Was my long-term planning adequate? What could I have done better?
What surprises did I get?
Has my weekly planning been adequate?

How have I evaluated my weekly plans?
Has my preparation and planning of daily work been adequate?
How have I monitored the daily outcomes?
With whom do I discuss daily teaching plans?
How does the classroom environment reflect the long-term, medium-term and short-term planning?
Do I share the long-term, medium-term and short-term plans with the pupils?
Have I learned anything about my ability to plan?
What are my main professional development needs in the area of planning?

Work with groups and individuals
To what extent do I match work to the needs of individuals?
What special provision have I made for the three highest achievers and the three lowest achievers in my class?
How do I monitor my use of time?
Have I successfully matched my teaching style to the needs and interests of pupils?
What are my strengths and weaknesses in knowledge, skill and interest?
To what extent does the work actually done match what I planned?
Do the pupils know what I expect of them?
What are my main professional development needs in the area of teaching groups and individuals?

TYPES OF PROFESSIONAL DEVELOPMENT

Professional development can take a number of forms. It has traditionally been seen as attending courses. Teachers spend a day or more out of school, or go in the evening or at weekends to a training provider such as a university or college. More recently a number of private organizations have joined the ranks of providers and many local education authorities have their own teams of trainers, usually advisory teachers.

Longer-term courses have usually led to a further qualification and moves are being made to enable teachers to gain accreditation for school-related work. This is a bridge between the traditional award-bearing course and the more recent development of school-based in-service training. This is based on the belief that the staff of a school contains a wide range of expertise and the idea is to spread that knowledge around the school.

Where a school feels it does not have particular expertise or it needs an infusion of fresh ideas or an informed outside view of its practices then it will call for the services of a consultant. These may be a school adviser, an advisory teacher, a colleague from another school or from a college or university. There are two facets to the outside consultant, as Smith (1996) has pointed out. On the one hand, it is important that schools have the self-confidence to seek advice from outside, on the other, the consultant should not be seen as the fount of all wisdom. Too often when faced with a difficult child or lacking expertise in a particular area there will be demands to call in an expert. As many schools are at the cutting edge of developments it is unrealistic to think that there will be someone out there who has the answers.

The Numeracy Project (DfEE, 1999) combines these several types of training into a package for schools. Initially it brings together head teachers and mathematics coordinators from a number of schools and familiarizes them with the aims of the Numeracy Project and its supporting materials. Having explained the National Numeracy Strategy the focus moves to making the strategy work for children in a particular school. Members of the project team visited schools and, together with the head teacher and mathematics coordinator, worked with them on auditing the current state of mathematics teaching in their schools. Having defined the strengths and weaknesses of the school's mathematics curriculum they together decided on priorities and drew up an action plan. Schools continued to receive support, as described in Chapter 7, but the focus of training moved to the school and became the responsibility of the head teacher and mathematics coordinator.

EVALUATING PROFESSIONAL DEVELOPMENT

The evaluation of training events is not something that should be sprung upon teachers when they return from a course but should be part of the learning process that begins with the application. The self-review described above will have established their current knowledge and their reasons for attending. They should also be sure of what they want to gain from the course. Course providers will relate stories of people being sent on a course at the last minute and not being properly prepared. The course tutor may have asked participants to do some preparation before the course and they were unaware of this requirement. The target audience might be mathematics coordinators and then the person who attends is disappointed because the tutor did not address his classroom needs.

Having ensured that the course description is appropriate and relevant to their management or teaching needs, and many substitute delegates have difficulty with this, the participants will attend and probably complete an evaluation sheet on what they thought of the course.

Evaluation should not stop at that point. On return to school they should discuss with a colleague their reaction to the course and what they learned from it. A few weeks later they should meet again and discuss how the course has helped them do their job better. Finally, they should consider the benefits to the school and to their children of attending the course.

INCLUSIVE STAFF DEVELOPMENT

Before moving on to the style and content of school-focused training, it might be worth considering how a national or local project involving mainstream and special schools might be a vehicle for promoting inclusive practices.

The term 'inclusion' refers to a broader concept than school placement and regards the mathematics curriculum as being applicable to all pupils, wherever they are. The National Curriculum in the UK applies to special as well as mainstream schools and making this a reality has involved adjustments and the development of appropriate teaching strategies (Robbins, 1991a). Bringing together the experiences gained by teachers in both special and mainstream schools has the potential for blending currently fragmented teaching techniques into a consistent and effective strategy.

Beveridge (1998) speaks of the need for well-planned, collaborative learning activities to encourage a move from what she sees as the current position where many children with special needs experience learning alongside their peers, not learning with them. Florian (1988) continues this theme by stating that inclusion, by definition, requires participation. This places an onus on the teacher to take active steps to promote inclusion. Her experience of establishing integration activities for pupils with severe learning difficulties (SLD) highlighted certain critical features, which were:

- The ways people work together to adapt the curriculum
- Attitudes towards pupils with learning difficulties
- Concern about social and academic outcomes.

Reference was made earlier to the benefits that can accrue from teachers in special education working with mainstream colleagues. It is essential that every opportunity is taken to promote joint working which has proved to be an effective way of producing 'joined-up thinking'. The Numeracy Strategy is one such opportunity and the evidence to date suggests that, to some extent, the opportunity has been taken. The principles and guidance of the Framework for Numeracy (DfEE, 1999) may be compatible with inclusion but some of the implementation strategies may not. It is clear that the intention has been to avoid the mistakes in implementing the National Curriculum which was delayed in special schools for a year, thereby giving the message that the authorities had not 'got their act together' with regard to special education. It also reinforced the commonly held view that special education was synonymous with special schools.

Taking Beveridge's (1998) principle of learning *with* rather than learning *alongside* it seems right to enshrine this principle in the preparation of teachers to implement the strategy. It would demonstrate a commitment from the government and local education authorities to include all children in the curriculum and it would demonstrate the readiness to support teachers in making their lessons meaningful to every child. It would send a clear message that this time a national initiative had truly inclusive values and would be an example to teachers, pupils, parents, governors and the whole community that individual differences did not preclude particular children from participating fully in the mainstream of education.

Some local education authorities have trained special school and mainstream teachers together, others have set up parallel training events. Those taking the second route have missed a golden opportunity by not structuring their training as a fully collaborative process. In the light of pressure from central government, it is understandable that those responsible for the training should want to avoid negative reactions from teachers of more able children who might feel held back by having to consider the pacing necessary for the lower-attaining pupils. Teachers from special schools might feel constrained from exploring the strategies they would use with children with complex, and in some cases profound, difficulties in learning. They would feel that their needs as teachers differed and that primary school colleagues would be discussing realms of mathematics, particularly in Key Stage 2, that, as one said, 'our children won't reach in a million years!' Even within special education, the varying performance of children with different types of disability will make any generalization questionable.

So the gulf to be bridged is not only one of content and pace, it is one of expectations. Challenging expectations leaves one open to accusations of being unrealistic, of not having taught these children, or of not appreciating the realities of the special school classroom. All these criticisms are understandable, but to accept them is not to condone them. They are not permanent absolutes, children have exceeded expectations, as the head teacher of a school for children with severe learning difficulties discovered when she saw her pupils working in a primary school.

The further along the continuum from high to low achievement one moves, and the more this is associated with certain disabling conditions, the greater the need to approach teaching in a specific, targeted way. To gain any impression of progress means breaking down the content into much smaller steps. This is quite acceptable in the Numeracy Framework, but not something that most mainstream teachers would see as being necessary.

COMFORT ZONES

Even when joint training sessions have been arranged there is a natural tendency to drift apart into the comfort zones of 'specials' and 'mainstreams'. The danger is that this drift will perpetuate traditional practices for children with individual needs rather than promote a breakthrough in teaching them. The principle of a common curriculum will be diluted and an alternative curriculum will arise by default.

There are considerable difficulties in writing a curriculum that encompasses relevant and meaningful learning outcomes for all children, including the most multiply disabled, and the more prescriptive the form of the curriculum the more challenging this becomes. It is perfectly justifiable to recognize the tension between the current and lifetime needs of someone who is deaf, blind and physically disabled with those of a bright, able child destined for university. There are sound arguments for differentiating the curriculum in a quite significant manner. None the less, this should not lead to a ceiling on expectations, as Christy Brown and Stephen Hawking demonstrate. These are indeed two exceptional human beings whose talents were realized long before 'inclusion' became a buzzword. The chances of one of the pupils in a special school demonstrating such a stunning intellect as these two is remote. In terms of the majority of people with such disabling conditions, the curriculum that has been developed in special schools is a realistic preparation for the highly dependent lifestyle that they will follow. It is perhaps at this point worth remembering that in the majority of countries children with that degree of disability, and many with a milder degree, have been outside the education system. None the less, we must remain alert to those indications, however slight, of potential exceeding that of the majority of children in a special school or unit.

Whilst the extremes can be used as arguments against the practice of inclusion, as we move further along the continuum of achievement those arguments become progressively weaker, with the exception of those with emotional and behavioural difficulties. Goodwins (1999) describes how two children in her school had to be excluded shortly following a change of teacher. The previous teacher, who had been the school's SENCO, had used strategies to contain the boys' behaviour but the new teacher, although competent, had not had the benefit of training in behaviour management strategies.

The general conclusion is that, having taken account of the challenges, achieving an inclusive ethos requires all involved in education to reconsider the role of the teacher (Florian, 1998). Whilst this extends beyond mathematics education, new approaches in the teaching of the subject should be based on inclusive principles and should keep those principles firmly in mind during the implementation phase.

TEACHING STYLES IN SPECIAL SCHOOLS

Training should address the differences in curriculum delivery between special and mainstream schools and search for strategies to help pupils through the culture shock of moving back into mainstream education. Both mainstream and special schools should be willing to adapt their strategies in the light of what they learn about teaching approaches used in both types of school.

Ainscow (1997) has pointed out that it might not be right to import special school practices into mainstream schools, but it might prove enlightening for mainstream teachers to be aware of those practices and why they have been developed. Teachers in the mainstream and special sectors can learn from one another and a convergence of thinking has the potential to benefit many more children than those designated SEN (Ainscow *et al.*, 1999).

KNOWLEDGE AND FUNCTIONAL SKILLS

Building on children's prior knowledge presupposes being able to identify what they already know, which may not be synonymous with what they can do. Children may solve an equation correctly by applying learned rules but not understand what they have done. Alternatively they may give an incorrect response despite understanding the procedure. The ability to make these distinctions can be developed with the support of teachers whose expertise lies in meeting individual needs.

A staff development programme will include input from colleagues such as the SENCO or learning support teacher and will relate the techniques of observation to the everyday classroom work of teachers and assistants. If possible, the training provider should have spent time in classes before the training session so that the course content has an immediate relevance and should follow up the course with further joint classroom work.

The course should include the modelling of good lessons and practice with versatile teaching strategies.

An open and trusting atmosphere is an essential prerequisite, so that teachers are not afraid to admit their own concerns and weaknesses.

The following example is of a training day provided for a special school. It is included as it illustrates many of the points about training and differentiation that are valid across the whole of primary education. It is envisaged that primary and special schools planning such training events might find it useful to draw upon the issues raised in this report rather than regard it as a model to be replicated without modification. As this was an interactive day, and in order to make this report more readable, the tutor's input and the participants' responses have been blended into a single narrative.

WHOLE-SCHOOL TRAINING DAY

A training day was run for the teachers and learning support assistants of a special school for primary-aged children with moderate learning difficulties. It was planned as a combination of input, discussion and group work. The intention was to follow, as far as possible the whole-class review – group work – plenary model so that the participants would become familiar with it.

We began the first session with an ice-breaker that explored people's feelings about mathematics. It was explained that as the tutor did not know the class he needed to establish a baseline from which to work. This was not intended to show anyone up but to recognize that many people have been daunted by mathematics. It is not surprising that teachers and support assistants who had a less than positive experience of learning mathematics should feel concerned about teaching the subject, particularly in primary mainstream and special schools where they have a responsibility to deliver the whole, or at least most, of the school's curriculum.

Participants were asked to rate themselves on the following scale:

- Level One: uncomfortable with the idea of teaching maths.
- Level Two: comfortable, but unsure of where activities fit into the sequence of learning.
- Level Three: a basic understanding of the process of learning mathematics but limited knowledge of strategies to make it interesting.

- Level Four: not unduly perturbed if someone comes into the classroom during a maths lesson.
- Level Five: pleased to involve visitors in the maths lesson; a source of ideas and support for other teachers.

There is usually a spread of self-assessments, and after discussion most people will agree to raise their own rating. The points that arise from this are:

- Self-assessment ratings are very rigorous.
- Many have a greater facility than they thought.
- Some report that their feelings about mathematics changed with a change of teacher.
- The children in our class are likely to have a similar range of feelings.
- We must be aware that we transmit our own feelings to our class.

We then considered Kipling's poem:

> I keep six honest serving-men,
> (They taught me all I knew);
> Their names are What and Why and When
> And How and Where and Who.
>> (R. Kipling *Just So Stories*, London:
>> Macmillan and Co., 1926)

WHAT SHOULD WE TEACH

For teachers in the UK the content is laid down in the National Curriculum. There are Programmes of Study for the age groupings 5–7 years of age (Key Stage 1) and 7–11 years of age (Key Stage 2). At Key Stage 1 there are three strands:

- Number
- Shape
- Space and Measures.

At Key Stage 2 there are four strands:

- Number
- Shape
- Space and Measures
- Handling Data.

The National Numeracy Strategy prescribes a lesson format and promotes a particular style of teaching, with an emphasis on mental and oral methods.

It prescribes a daily lesson of 45 minutes and sets out key objectives and a programme for each year. So we have gone from a desired outcome at the end of each key stage to a prescription of what is to be expected each year. The yearly teaching programme has planning grids to show how the mathematical topics can be grouped into units of work for each year. For example in Year 1 (6-year-olds) children are expected within *Number* to be able to:

- Count at least 20 objects
- Count on and back in ones from any small number, and in tens from and back to zero.

In Year 3 (8-year-olds) they would be expected to:

- Read and write whole numbers to at least 1000
- Recognise unit fractions such as ½, ¼, etc.

This immediately presents a problem to the teacher of children with learning difficulties who knows that very few, if any, children in the class would make that degree of progress in two years. This is recognized in the Framework for Numeracy: 'Special schools are encouraged to adopt the framework but should also adapt arrangements to suit their particular circumstances'; and it is suggested that in such circumstances teachers should plan an extended timescale for achieving the learning goals. This might mean taking two years to cover one year's learning goals so that work for six years of primary education in a special school would be based on what teachers in mainstream education would normally expect to cover in three years.

This is realistic and teachers in special schools welcome this flexibility as enabling them to include their children in the Numeracy Strategy. It does, however, raise an issue for when children move from special schools into mainstream primary schools in that they may not have covered some of the topics that their new class is already familiar with.

TEACHING MATERIALS

Whilst teaching materials are provided as part of the Numeracy Strategy they will not be sufficient to cover the wide range of resources needed for a class that has children working at a much wider range of levels than would be expected in a mainstream class. The teacher will have to look carefully at suggested learning tasks and materials to see if they need to be adapted to make them appropriate for children who are older than those for whom they were designed. Above all, it demonstrates that any such presentation of learning goals is at best schematic and cannot represent the often archaic and disorganized way that people learn nor take account of the peaks and troughs of knowledge which characterize the performance of children with learning difficulties.

Teachers also expressed concern about the kind of assessment tools, including the UK National Curriculum Standard Assessment Tasks for 7- and 11-year-olds, which measure whether an answer is right or wrong but do not give credit either for the process of achieving the correct result or the progress the child is making towards understanding the concepts involved in solving the problem.

The tests are often presented in written form and this will disadvantage those with limited reading ability. The tasks presented in verbal form will depend upon the children having the appropriate vocabulary and this may prevent them from understanding a problem that involves skills that, mathematically, they may well possess.

Behaviour and attention span will also affect children's performance and these factors in combination do lead to the concern that tests assess children's ability to perform well in assessment situations but do not necessarily give a true indication of their knowledge and skills. It has also to be asked whether if the same task was presented in a way that was meaningful to them they might perform better. Differentiation is built into these tests and alternative communication methods can be used for those with sensory difficulties but it is debatable whether differences in learning style or characteristics are taken into account sufficiently to enable all children to demonstrate the extent of their mathematical understanding. The tests might show whether their answers are correct or incorrect but they do not always indicate the extent to which they might be nearly correct. Such snapshot measures may serve as an indication of the relative progress of a cohort of children across the whole education system but they have limited value as aids to improving the achievement of the lowest-attaining children.

Teachers felt that there could be a tension between the expectations on them to include all children in the full curriculum and the personal needs of children as identified in their individual education plans. A child needing regular physiotherapy might have to receive this outside the classroom and miss all or part of a lesson. Schools have resolved this problem by ensuring that the physiotherapist is present during physical education lessons or sees the child at a time that does not disrupt their curriculum timetable.

When a child has an ongoing need for particular types of support or behaviour management, the normal flow of teaching may be difficult to maintain and this is harder to predict and plan for. The potential for distractibility present in a class of children with moderate learning difficulties, many of whom also had associated emotional and behavioural problems, was considered a reason for adapting the lesson format prescribed in the Framework for Numeracy by not having a final plenary session.

The framework refers to the plenary session as an important part of the lesson in which the teacher can help the children 'assess their developing knowledge against any targets they have been set and to see for themselves the progress they are making'. It may be that after receiving the Numeracy training teachers might have a clearer idea of how they could use a plenary session and build it into their planning. The potential benefits of providing the kind of review of learning described in the Framework need to be weighed against the demands they might make on classroom management. Earlier comments about children learning the routines might well be applicable.

The framework presents the learning objectives in yearly blocks. Teachers felt that it would be more useful to have them presented in one overall chart as they would need to draw out objectives for several years to cover the range of achievement in their class. In the Framework for Numeracy it is suggested that, for classes with several age groups, content of their lessons during a year would span several years and proposes that teachers adapt the planning grid for one year to cover the whole class, by drawing objectives from the other year, or that they design their own. Teachers in the special school felt that an overall chart would facilitate this approach to planning.

Where

We considered questions such as:

- Is the classroom the best place to learn mathematics?
- What maths can be learned in the playground?
- What maths can be learned in the gym?
- What maths can be used in assembly?

Who

In terms of the children we made clear an intention to include everyone. This also applied to the adults working in the classroom, whose training needs should be identified and included in the staff development programme.

Why

This is the question we often do not have time to ask and yet without this mathematics teaching becomes a race through a series of hoops put there by someone else. The result is an uninspiring plod from one learning goal to the next that will lead to some children having that same dread of the subject that we spoke of earlier.

Mathematics the servant

We took the five strands of the Numeracy Framework:

- Number and the number system

- Calculations
- Solving problems
- Measures, shape and space
- Handling data

and considered how these mathematical functions were used in everyday life.

Mathematics the citizen

We considered how mathematical functions enable children to develop their knowledge and skills in other areas of the curriculum.

Mathematics the sovereign

We reminded ourselves of the pleasure that can be gained from mathematically related activities at all levels, from shape and patterns, stories and maths trails to the mind-bending puzzles such as Rubik's cube.

Mathematics that is meaningful and relevant

We considered the way mathematics was currently taught in the school and what were the strengths of that approach. This was then related to the Framework for Numeracy and we considered its implications for the school's mathematics education.

Planning and evaluating the teaching of mathematics

This was followed by an workshop session in which teaching teams looked in more detail at what was expected of the age group they taught and what adaptations they would need to implement to make those learning goals relevant for their children.

Evaluation

The Framework for Numeracy (DfEE, 1999) puts forward a number of factors that make it applicable to special schools. These were listed and the staff were asked to judge whether these factors were either well established in the school, at an embryonic stage (growth points) or not present. The latter were expressed as possible targets for development and the group looked at how the growth points could be developed to achieve those targets.

TALKING POINT

How do you identify your personal professional needs?

12

Resources for teaching and learning

commercial mathematics materials have much to offer
. . . as a source of ideas for teachers to use, develop and extend.

(Millett *et al.*, 1995)

CREATING A LEARNING ENVIRONMENT

The first thing that catches your attention on entering a school is the quality of the visual environment. You start with a positive view when you go into a school that has obviously given a lot of thought and attention to providing interesting displays. The entrance hall gives an indication of the importance the school places on keeping parents and visitors informed about its work. As you move around the school you will become aware of the school curriculum and build up an image of how it is taught.

The informed observer will soon be able to judge the age group being taught by the content of the displays. Teachers of young children believe that they will be motivated to learn in classrooms that have been planned and resourced to enable them to exercise a degree of choice in what they do next. As one nursery head teacher said, 'The environment is the third adult in the classroom.' This can be informative for parents and visitors, such as a display in the entrance hall on what the school is aiming to achieve and an outline of the teaching programmes.

In the classroom the teacher will have arranged the furniture to create the kind of learning environment that is considered most appropriate for the particular age group. The emphasis for younger children will be on creating accessible opportunities to learn, through investigation, exploration, interaction with displays or practical tasks that have a definite learning outcome. As they progress through the primary school the nature of the classroom environment will change, expressing their growing maturity and the style of teaching being used. For some children with individual needs this may be challenging as they still need the opportunities to explore in practical activities that are no longer considered appropriate for the majority of the class.

An inclusive classroom will reflect this diversity of maturity in a manner that is sensitive to the child's self-esteem. In some instances it may be necessary to move the child on to working with the resources used by the rest of the children in the class. The teacher and the learning support assistant will be alert to signs of a negative reaction that might result in a barrier being created to the child's participation in the class.

SHARING RESOURCES

At a workshop session for teachers from primary and special schools the participants all brought along examples of teaching materials they had found or had made themselves and in this way good ideas can be disseminated very quickly. Undoubtedly the best materials are those tried and tested in the classroom. Some of the best are those made by teachers and assistants and this is particularly true of materials made for differentiating what the whole class is using so that is meaningful to children with individual needs.

This is, however, time-consuming and we have already recognized how valuable is the time that teachers have for review and professional development. There has to be, therefore, a strong reliance on materials produced by publishers.

CHOOSING MATERIALS

Before describing the different types of material that are available we will consider a few general points about choosing materials.

Firstly, have all members of staff who will have to use those materials been involved in the decision to buy them? Many schools find themselves having to use schemes and apparatus that the head teacher or mathematics coordinator were impressed by at an exhibition or on a visit to another school. When put into use in the classroom the rest of the staff find that their enthusiasm was misplaced and that they themselves need alternative or supplementary materials for their class. Unfortunately, a great deal of money has already been invested and there is none available to provide what they see as desirable, or even essential, items for their children.

They might try to persuade the SENCO to use special needs funds to buy the materials but that, too, is limited. It does also raise the question about whether the purchasing decision took account of individual needs. It must also be asked whether any material under consideration:

- supports, incorporates, or is compatible with, the balance between practical activities, oral and mental activities and recording
- has written material of a readability level suitable for all children in the class and, if not, what has been done to make it accessible
- takes account of age-appropriateness
- has a balance between the different aspects of mathematics and makes explicit connections between the various strands
- has recommendations for alternative materials
- has clear explanations
- has materials that can be used in a flexible way
- is interesting and motivates the children to want to use it.

TYPES OF MATERIALS

A well-resourced school will have a range of materials that can be used in mathematics teaching. These will include written materials such as maths schemes, topic books, reference books, workbooks, workcard schemes, supplementary cards, worksheets and posters.

Practical materials include: mathematical apparatus, structural apparatus, games and puzzles, domestic and natural objects and playground equipment.

Technological equipment includes: calculators, audio tapes, video cassettes, overhead projectors, slide projectors, television programmes and computer programmes.

They can be obtained from a number of publishers and bought either through their catalogues or at exhibitions and displays at conferences. Some examples are given but this does not represent an exhaustive list of what is available.

Maths schemes

There are many commercial mathematics schemes and, where there is a national or other form of statutory curriculum, publishers will ensure the marketability of their products by showing clear links with its requirements. Harris and Henkhuzens (1998) found that schools in England had a high level of reliance on these schemes.

Publishers have successfully promoted the idea that maths can be taught through schemes and then failed, inevitably, to publish schemes that met everyone's needs. Schemes will not meet teachers' needs in full because every teacher has a different level and type of background knowledge, differing amounts of confidence in teaching maths, different levels of personal mathematical competence, different understanding of the process of learning mathematics and different appreciation of how that process can break down in the minds of individual children.

They will not meet pupils' needs because every pupil comes to learning with a unique body of mathematical knowledge. Even if the mathematical content is within the child's grasp, they may not be able to perform the tasks because they cannot read the text in which the problem is presented.

The Numeracy Strategy is intended to move the focus of mathematical education away from textbook and printed schemes towards an oral, interactive approach. Publishers are responding by producing large format books ('big books') that can be used in whole-class lessons.

Workbooks and workcard schemes

O'Toole and O'Toole (1989) came to the conclusion that children with learning difficulties need a series of finely graded preparatory steps. In recent years publishers have produced supplementary materials for low-attaining children within their schemes. This would give them an experience of success, and the Mathsteps materials (Robbins, 1996) are an example of a structured set of activities intended to help teachers bridge the gap between the expectations of the first two years of formal education and the difficulties faced by pupils who have not achieved those levels within the expected time-span. They give guidance on appropriate activities to develop the underpinning knowledge and skills required by the National Curriculum and can be used by learning support assistants for individual or group work with young children needing additional support and throughout the primary age range with those needing regular individual support.

Topic books and reference books

These can be specifically designed to cover particular mathematical topics for certain age ranges. The written and skill content may be appropriate for older children with special needs but the interest level and context may not.

General topic books and stories can be used as the inspiration for mathematical investigations. The advantage of this kind of material is that the teacher has more scope to adapt the activity to the ability and interests of the group.

Materials that have been successfully used in this approach include train, bus and cross-channel ferry timetables.

Worksheets

The mathematical experiences of many children with learning difficulties have centred around worksheets. Some were commercially produced by specialized publishers, others were duplicated sheets of rows of simple equations, typed or handwritten, produced by teachers. The availability of desktop publishing programmes has led to a considerable improvement in the quality of school-produced materials but it still begs the question as to whether this type of material is overused. The Cockroft Report (DES, 1982) emphasized the need for a balance between practical, oral and written work but, for many children with individual needs, mathematics remained a predominantly written activity.

Mathematical apparatus

Classrooms should be equipped with apparatus for measuring height, length, distance and weight. There should be jugs and cylinders for measuring volume and capacity and a frame made up of metre rules gives an immediate visual image of a cubic metre.

There should be an accurate clock and other materials that can be used in practical activities for measuring time differences and the passage of time.

Publishers' catalogues contain a wealth of materials. Some may be purchased as a permanent classroom resource while others could be in a central resource accessible to the classes that might find the most use for them.

Structural apparatus

Unit blocks, such as multilink, that fit together to make rods are popular items and provide a concrete representation of number values for those children whose ability to calculate mentally is not yet secure. There are larger blocks available and these may be better for children with poor fine motor skills.

There is increasing interest in the abacus as a means of learning counting and computational skills. Hatano (1997) considers that learning how to operate an abacus helps the development of the concept of place value and an understanding of written calculation procedures.

Games and puzzles

Newton (1999) considers games to be a motivating and stress-free way for children with individual needs to develop a positive attitude towards mathematics and to consolidate their learning. She gives examples of number games that could be used in a group work session and could also be put in 'take-home packs' for parents and children to use at home.

The games used at home do not have to be specially designed mathematical games. Card games, draughts, chess and chequers all provide opportunities to use number words and mathematical concepts.

Domestic and natural objects

The head teacher of a nursery school had been to visit schools in Italy and was impressed by the arrangement they had to obtain scrap materials for classroom use from a central resource. She had found a similar source and was establishing a resource base containing items such as carpet pieces, cut-out shapes, corks, bottle tops, plastic containers and anything else that could be used for practical activities. Parents were encouraged to take out materials on loan and they were given ideas on activities they could do at home with their children.

Playground equipment

Mention has been made of maths trails and the school playground is an ideal place to establish one. Activity packs can be prepared and added to by staff when they devise a new activity.

Calculators

There has been considerable debate about the desirability of introducing calculators to young children. There is a need to ensure that they learn the skills of estimating so that they can have an idea of what the answer should be. Having said that, most young children will find them fascinating and it is hard to imagine a household with older siblings that does not have some lying around.

Audio tapes

Where children's reading ability has hindered their progress on written activity cards teachers have used recorded tapes to give them additional support. The wearing of headphones will also cut out extraneous distractions and help the child to concentrate.

Video cassettes and television programmes

These can bring a fresh and lively material to mathematics teaching if used selectively. It is important that the teacher has reviewed the tape so that additional support can be arranged for children who might find it difficult to follow the development of the lesson.

Computer programmes

The range and amount of software is increasing rapidly and it would not be helpful to attempt to give an inventory of what is available as that would be very soon out of date. Again, teachers need to view the software so that they can plan how it can be used by children at different levels of achievement. Many programmes are accompanied by related worksheets and record sheets.

Often children use computers alone but teachers should consider how children can work together on activities. Partnering a low-attaining child with a higher-attaining one may be helpful to both. The former will benefit from support and the latter will reinforce his learning through explaining the process.

Maths weeks

A week with a whole-school focus on mathematics gives an opportunity for raising awareness of what can be learned from the school environment. Indoor maths trails that require children to interact with materials and displays by answering questions or performing a practical task make the subject 'come alive' and create a sense of partnership in learning. A 'room number trail' will involve children finding out and recording the numbers on the doors of specified rooms in the school. A 'shapes' trail could involve finding shapes that occur as part of the building; rectangles on doors, circles on clocks and so on; or be set up with different shapes stuck on walls and boards.

Children can be involved in the planning of the week by putting forward ideas and bringing objects and information from home and by producing publicity materials.

Parents can be invited to undertake the activities set up around the school and the programme for the week can also include workshops for them to learn more about the teaching of mathematics. Children can act as guides and mentors, and the process of explaining to parents will help to consolidate their own learning.

The aim of the week can be to celebrate mathematics and there should be events during the week when every child can show what they have achieved.

TALKING POINTS

Do you have a range of materials in the school to support oral, mental, written and practical activities?
Does every child have access to material suitable for his or her current stage of learning?

13

Recognizing inclusive practices

The key issues . . . are how children can share common experiences
to fulfil a variety of learning experiences, and how to ensure that the teaching
approaches are flexible enough to allow for a varied style of learning.

(CSIE, 1996)

EVALUATING INCLUSIVE PRACTICES

We have set out in Chapter 1 some principles for inclusive
mathematics and considered in Chapter 5 what those mean in
practice. We now turn our attention to judging whether those
principles have been established in a school and the extent to which
they create conditions for effective teaching and learning.

The work of schools is subject to regular inspection in most
countries. A full inspection will cover all subjects on the curriculum
whereas a focused inspection will look at one or two particular aspects
of the curriculum. This approach has been used to make judgements
on the effectiveness of mathematics teaching across a number of
schools. A survey of the teaching of number in three local education
authorities (Ofsted, 1997) expressed concern at the standards being
achieved with comments such as 'in a third of schools long term
planning in number was inadequate to ensure progression'. This kind
of survey has its value at the policy level and may result in additional
resources being targeted at those schools, as was the case with the
Numeracy Project, but to translate those resources into improved
achievement requires action at the school level.

It is the implementation of school improvement measures that will
achieve the goal of raising standards and it is essential, if a school is to
be inclusive, that the principles of inclusion are incorporated into
development planning.

PLANNING FOR INCLUSIVE MATHEMATICS

Planning is the first stage in achieving a goal. If planning is to be
relevant it must begin with a recognition of what is the intended
outcome of the process. If we take the principles established earlier;

> A mathematics curriculum that encompasses the *needs, expecta-
> tions* and *aspirations* of all pupils, that *motivates* them and *enriches*
> their school experience,

then future action is grounded in a clear view that the goal is a full
education for every child that is entitled to attend the school. For a
school that serves a local community that means every child in that
community. The school will have other policies in terms of special
needs, acceptable behaviour and admissions from outside the area that
will qualify that entitlement but for an inclusive school individual
learning needs will not be one. It is an unequivocal statement that the
school will be aiming to provide a high-quality mathematical
education for every child.

CURRICULUM AUDIT

The school will be regularly reviewing its work. In terms of
mathematics it will have made an audit of the curriculum to ensure
that statutory requirements are being met, that the curriculum is being
delivered in each class and that targets from individual education
plans are being incorporated into the planned curriculum. Members of
staff will be collectively alert to opportunities for furthering the
process of inclusion, aware of the impediments to access, both
physical ones within the building and attitudinal ones within the
larger community of the school. It will have clear proposals for
tackling both sets of issues and will have established means of
minimizing their effect until solutions have been found.

The school will have procedures for auditing its mathematics
curriculum. This might involve the mathematics coordinator sitting in
on lessons either to gain an overall view or to study the performance
of particular children. Whatever the purpose, the coordinator will have
discussed the visit beforehand with the class teacher and the focus of
the observation will have been agreed then. At the earliest possible
opportunity after the lesson the coordinator will have a further
discussion with the teacher.

An observation might be made by the SENCO and the focus then is
likely to be on meeting the needs of individual children. This can be
followed up by the class teacher meeting with the two coordinators
and discussing how to ensure that all the children are receiving the full
range of curriculum experiences. They can together analyse the
teacher's planning documents, lesson evaluation notes and children's
individual education plans.

When observing individual children they might decide to pay close
attention to their participation, to the time spent on task or to their
positive and negative responses to activities and to the classroom

environment. It will also be an opportunity to evaluate differentiated approaches and materials and to decide on further work in these areas. This might take the form of curriculum development work with colleagues or professional development for the teacher or learning support assistant.

The willingness to learn will be a key feature of a staff that is committed to inclusion and meetings will be characterized by frequent reference to what members of staff have read, learned on a course or seen at another school. No idea will be dismissed and everyone's contribution will be regarded as a stepping stone to developing collective knowledge. The pervading ethos will be of a learning environment for every member of the school community.

OBSERVATION

Taking on the role of a visitor to the school we will consider ways of evaluating the extent to which the principles of inclusive mathematics are established.

The entrance hall will have told us a lot about the value the staff put on the school environment. Some schools have a display with the aims of the school and photographs of children doing activities that relate to those aims. For example, a school that teaches mathematics through a balance of oral and practical experiences had pictures of children carrying out a measuring activity and another of an oral maths lesson with the teacher using a metre ruler segmented into ten coloured parts as the basis for the lesson.

The aims of the school will make reference to the school's inclusive principles and displays of children's work will include some from lower-attaining children.

On entering the classroom, the first impression will be of purposeful activity. The children may be so intensely occupied that they will not even notice a visitor coming into the room. It will soon become clear if the room is organized to take account of individual requirements and whether the staff are conversant with the considerations that have to be made for particular types of special need.

The visitor will note if the displays are at the children's viewing height, if they engage the children's interest and whether they are designed to be accessible to every pupil in terms of interest, presentation and readability.

During the lesson the visitor will note if the teacher uses praise and encouragement, and corrects children's work in a constructive manner. The teacher's response to children's work will indicate whether the focus is on comparing them against the rest of the class or on individuals surpassing their own previous achievements.

The results of assessment will be presented in a way that celebrates the progress of lower-attaining children as part of the overall success of the school. Teachers will recognize the shortcomings of assessment methods and have alternative evidence that gives credit to those whose progress through the stages of learning is slower than that of the majority.

COMPETITION

It is inevitable that even if the teacher does not introduce an element of competition, the children, and probably their parents, will. When competition is used as a motivator it should not be done in a way that diminishes the achievements of the low attainer. It must always be made clear that reaching personal goals is more important than being 'top of the class'. The fable of the hare and the tortoise might be used to illustrate this point.

THE HIGH-ENERGY INCLUSIVE CLASSROOM

We discussed earlier the features of a 'high-energy classroom': Pace; Know-how; Investigating, conjecturing and proving; and Struggle. We will now consider some of the characteristics of a high-energy *inclusive* classroom.

Pace

The teacher keeps the lesson moving and has the ability to run the lesson so that all the children are kept involved. Like the differential gear on a car that adjusts to the variation in speed on the wheels when cornering, this teacher has 'differential gears', adjusting the pace throughout the lesson in response to the reactions of different children in the class. This can mean operating on occasions at three speeds; overdrive for the more able, a low gear for the slower learners and a gear in between to keep the lesson moving for the majority of the class. Other adults working in the classroom understand what is happening and complement the teacher's input by seeing which children need support and giving it as soon as possible.

Know-how

The teacher knows the process of mathematical learning and uses strategies to help children overcome obstacles that might hinder their progress. Classroom support is targeted at enabling children to participate in the lesson and the staff concerned are well briefed on their role and the content of the lesson.

Investigating, conjecturing and proving

The children with individual needs take part in investigational work and the teacher has planned the tasks so that they can make a meaningful contribution. This may entail preparing additional materials that set a task within the main topic but at a level appropriate for them.

Struggle

All the children in the class will be set tasks that they have to make an effort to achieve. The feature of an inclusive class will be the wide range of expectations being pursued. The teacher will have a high level of organizational skill and will be able to switch instantly from supporting a child who is struggling to extending one who is finding the task well within his or her capabilities.

PARENTAL VIEWS

We have seen the school through the eyes of an observer, whom we have probably assumed to be a fellow teacher. How differently would we view it if we were visiting as a parent?

No doubt we would wish to see the features described above but we would also want to be sure that our child was happy. The school may feel it is doing its duty by stretching every child but the parents might be getting a backlash in the form of an anxious or disturbed child.

Regular contact with parents is an essential feature of an inclusive school. The means of communication may not always be straightforward. Many children want to keep home and school separate and parents of children of all abilities have experienced an unwillingness on the part of their offspring to relate the day's events at school. This is not obstruction on the part of the children but a natural part of the growth of independence and it is encouraging to see this happening to a child designated as SEN. The school and the parents should not undermine this by insisting on sending messages or interrogating the child but, if they have concerns, should contact the school by telephone. They may feel that the school is demanding too much of their child and this concern should be discussed openly between them both.

Many schools will have taken steps to prevent this situation arising by having regular workshops for parents. Parents at one school wanted to know more about the mathematics curriculum so they ran 'Maths Workshops'. Then they discovered that some parents who they desperately wanted to be involved were reluctant to take part so they ran similar workshops but under the title 'playing games with children'. The lesson from this is that schools have, at times, to be imaginative in forging home–school links with the families who would benefit most. This is very much in line with the philosophy of including everyone in the 'family of the school'. By involving the parents of children who are at risk of underachieving in their educational career schools are taking a significant step in preventing school failure.

RECIPE FOR SUCCESS

These features are part of the recipe for success. The recipe for disaster, according to CSIE (1996) is:

- Inadequate liaison
- Incompatible aims, values or teaching styles
- Unwillingness to share control
- Communication problems.

No school is perfect and all will experience these problems to a lesser or greater degree. The difference lies in the willingness of the school to address these issues and for the mathematics curriculum that means:

- Good liaison on teaching strategies between colleagues in a supportive and progressive staffroom atmosphere.
- Relevant professional development that is part of the overall school development plan and is evaluated for its contribution towards achieving the aims of the school.
- A shared set of principles, such as those set out for inclusive mathematics.
- Trust between colleagues that can distinguish professional discourse from personal disagreement.
- Openness to new ideas.
- Openness to constructive criticism from sources within and outside the school.
- Contact with parents in terms that they can understand and from which they can gain a full picture of their child's progress towards short- and long-term learning targets.

CHILDREN'S EXPECTATIONS OF SCHOOLS

What do the principles of inclusive mathematics mean for the child with individual learning needs?

A broad and rich mathematical education

Their programme should cover all the strands of the school curriculum, with adaptations made to content and materials so that it is relevant to their present stage of learning and their future needs. They should be included in all aspects of the curriculum and not be restricted to the purely functional aspects. A classroom where some children worked for a large part of the lesson in isolation from the main class would still have some way to go before it could claim to be offering an inclusive mathematics curriculum.

Be expected to do better than their perceived best

There would be learning targets for every child, drawn from the mathematics curriculum framework. All staff working in the classroom would be aware of those targets and would be encouraging the child to achieve them. The classroom ethos would be one of 'support towards achievement' and every child would feel a commitment towards enabling everyone to achieve his or her best.

Participate in projects and initiatives aimed at improving the teaching and learning of mathematics

Schools that become involved in projects should be aiming to involve all the children in the target age group. Any project that requires children to meet selection criteria based on ability or achievement in order to participate should be approached with caution. Questions should be asked about the means available in the project for involving every child in a meaningful way.

Where projects are presented with a rhetoric of inclusion schools should ensure that the content and proposed working procedures make it possible for every child to gain something from the school's involvement.

Benefit from a flexible approach

Children's preferred learning styles may clash with the approach being used by the teacher. Teachers should recognize this and be prepared to adapt their presentation to utilize the child's capabilities rather than bemoan their inability to keep up with those who do respond to the teacher's style.

This flexibility must be consistent throughout the school and teachers brought in to cover staff absence should receive induction on the style of teaching that is being followed.

Have their achievements celebrated

What for some children may be a routine task will represent a major achievement for others. This calls for a differentiated response from the teacher so that the struggling child can feel the 'warm glow of success' and be motivated to further effort. This should be genuine recognition and should not be done either in a dismissive or in a patronizing way.

Benefit from their teachers having the confidence to identify their own strengths and weaknesses in teaching mathematics

Very few people are good at everything. Most of us ordinary mortals have areas in which we have a high degree of capability and a number of weak spots. The primary teacher having to deliver the whole curriculum for five days a week to the same children will not be equally strong in all of them.

For some their weakness lies in mathematics. Recognizing this is the first step to putting it right. Having admitted that 'my mathematics teaching is not as good as it should be' the teacher can then start a process of self-improvement.

Experience mathematics as an international language and use it as an effective means of communication with people beyond the school

An increasing number of schools have entered into partnerships with schools in other countries. The activities within the partnership often involve investigation and the exchange of information. No child should feel excluded from this type of activity and schools should ensure that the partnership agreement and the plan of action are designed to enable the involvement of all the children attending the school.

There is a growing body of experience on the participation of children with special educational needs in international partnerships (Bovair and Robbins, 1996) and these indicate the value of such activities to those who, at present it has to be said, are more likely to take part in them at special school than in mainstream education.

Benefit from an active commitment within the school and beyond that everyone is entitled to enjoy success in maths

The ethos of inclusion should permeate all elements of the school's daily life. The commitment to creating a learning environment that gives opportunities for every child to experience success should be made explicit regularly, not only through words but through the thousands of interpersonal interactions that occur each day.

PREVENTION OF LEARNING DIFFICULTIES

The school should be taking active measures to prevent children's problems becoming learning difficulties. Termly or annual assessments will identify certain children as 'below average' or 'failing'. Teachers will have been aware of the children's problems well before then and should be able to trigger an 'early warning system'.

This is a sensitive matter and less confident or less experienced teachers will feel that doing so might lead to them being seen as inadequate teachers. It is here that the mentor can be a sounding board and perhaps suggest a few ideas for the teacher to try. They might even recognize the problem as similar to one they and other colleagues have experienced. The support of teachers who have successfully dealt with this situation can then be enlisted.

Utilizing the experience and empathy of colleagues is the purpose of Teacher Support Teams (Creese *et al.*, 1997). These are school-based problem-solving groups to which teachers can bring their concerns. A support team for inclusive mathematics might be made up initially of the mathematics coordinator, the SENCO and another experienced class teacher who is confident in the subject. Teachers will state their concerns and the group will discuss ways that the group can support the teacher in finding a way forward. The important thing is that the problem becomes one for the whole group, not just for the teacher. Having been through this process and become more confident in teaching mathematics to the whole ability range the teacher may at a later stage be able to make a contribution his or herself as a member of the support team.

The concern expressed by a teacher may lead to a realization that this is an issue for an age group or even across the whole school. A proactive school will then take steps to find a collective solution through the school's development planning process.

INCLUSIVE PROCESS

Throughout this chapter we have been highlighting features to indicate whether the school's mathematics curriculum was inclusive. We have accepted that this will not be achieved overnight, if it ever is totally achievable, but move forward in the belief that the progressive development of increasingly inclusive practices will result in a reduction in educational failure.

Convincing evidence that the development of inclusive practices leads directly to the reduction of low attainment is not available. As with so much in the field of individual learning difficulties, we have to extrapolate from what has been found to be effective with the majority of children.

The report on the first year of the National Numeracy Project (Ofsted, 1998) noted that children with special educational needs benefited most from school's participation in the project. The marginalization of low-attaining children, noted before the project began, had been overcome through close working between the class teacher and the learning support assistant. However, the report does note that the best results had been achieved by grouping children into ability sets. This suggests that one aspect of effective practice actually runs counter to the principles of inclusion, which leads in turn to the question of whether the process of developing inclusive practices has to conform to the principles of inclusion.

TALKING POINT

What can we do in school to prevent children's problems becoming special educational needs?

14

Promoting inclusive mathematics

The complex process of adapting schools to diversity
cannot be conceptualised simply as a replacement of practices,
but as an innovative process of change at school level.

(Parrilla, 1999)

PRINCIPLES AND PRACTICE

We noted at the end of the last chapter that gains in numeracy were most marked when children were grouped according to ability. The Framework for Numeracy (DfEE, 1999) refers to 'controlled differentiation' which is understood to mean limiting the ability range within a class.

Graham and colleagues (1999), taking a Vygotskian view that children construct knowledge through social interaction with the teacher or their peers, compare an individualized approach to learning mathematics with the whole-class approach followed in Hungarian schools. They see that the teacher does more than identify individual attainment; he or she has to be aware of where the children are in relation to their understanding of the mathematics in question. The teacher's role is to move children from being able to perform mathematical tasks with assistance from an adult or peer to a stage where they can perform them independently (Knight, 1999).

Such an approach is facilitated by all the children in the class being at a similar stage and it should be noted that children in Hungary who experience difficulties in learning are removed from the main teaching group. There is an assumption that they will rejoin the class at some stage, but this will depend upon their ability to 'catch up' with the others. Whilst the principle of 'differentiated teaching' (Graham *et al.*, 1999), that is the teacher giving different levels of assistance to enable the whole class to work together, is in line with the approach to mathematics teaching currently being promoted, it does assume that the range of mathematical ability and understanding present in the class is within certain parameters. The Framework for Numeracy (DfEE, 1999) sets those parameters as being at most 'three levels of differentiation'.

DIFFERENTIATED OR DIFFERENT?

The idea of limiting the degree of differentiation raises the question whether it is realistic to have one mathematics curriculum for all children, whatever their ability or disability. Is there, in practical teaching terms, a need to draw a line between a differentiated version of the curriculum for the majority and an individual learning programme which varies considerably in content, style and methodology? In other words, when does *differentiated* become *different*?

Proponents of schools being fully inclusive would maintain that 'there is no teaching or caring in a segregated school which cannot take place in an ordinary school' and that schools should aim to 'provide a curriculum which is accessible and relevant to all pupils' (CSIE, 1996). This creates an expectation that mainstream schools provide an appropriate curriculum for every pupil, whatever the severity or complexity of their needs. The UK government seems to be adopting a more cautious line when referring to the development of 'a more inclusive framework' which implies that absolute inclusion remains a distant goal.

This is in line with the idea that inclusion is about the development of inclusive practice. The outcome will be a process characterized by redrawings of the lines so that more of the non-included become included. This is a more dynamic view of special needs than those that depend on a fixed threshold separating those in mainstream education from those in segregated placements. Fish (1984) referred to the future of special schools depending upon the ability of ordinary schools to cope with individual differences. This implies that mainstream schools will either adopt curricular practices used in special schools, taking note of Ainscow's (1997) caution about their transferability, or differentiate their curriculum to a much greater degree than at present. The work on low attainment in mathematics will be only one step in a major overhaul of pedagogy in mainstream schools. Yet that pedagogy is being influenced by other demands, including pressure to raise academic standards and to achieve higher examination pass rates.

The word 'unrealistic' crops up often in discussions on whether mainstream expectations should apply to children with SEN. This book is no exception and no apology is made. We cannot escape from the fact that there are children with conditions or circumstances that have resulted in them progressing at a much slower, at times hardly discernible, pace compared with the majority of children of their age. Just how far can we bend and stretch the mainstream curriculum to make it meaningful and relevant for them? There is a danger that the efforts of teachers will be expended in a semantic or cosmetic exercise to define the curriculum that best suits the children in their school in terms that would be recognizable to teachers in mainstream education.

On the other hand, to draw the line between the mainstream and an alternative curriculum too near to the normal level of achievement would deny many children the opportunities for an enriched curriculum that have been described earlier. By adopting strategies such as 'jig-sawing', where a group activity is broken down into smaller, interdependent parts (Marvin, 1998), children with a wide range of needs, including profound and multiple learning difficulties, can participate in a personally meaningful way.

CONTINUUM OF SUPPORT

Adult intervention with children who have difficulty in maintaining the pace of the majority can be viewed along a continuum from minimal support for a short time to high-density involvement over a prolonged period, which for some could be for the whole of their school career. It is feasible that children who benefit from minimal short-term support will be able to rejoin the mainstream. For those who take longer the likelihood is less, and will depend upon the extent to which they have kept in touch with both the pace and the content of the mathematics learning of the other children.

Thomas *et al.* (1998) consider that some children will require different educational experiences from others. Whilst there is merit in considering the curriculum 'not as knowledge to be conveyed but as a set of teaching and learning relationships by which that knowledge is conveyed' (Swann, 1988), it has to be recognized that the result of prescribing a standard curriculum is that the content becomes the curriculum. Talking with teachers of pupils with severe and profound learning difficulties, the writer found that there was considerable emphasis on 'what we are supposed to teach'. As prescription of methodology followed, teachers then felt uncomfortable about the relevance of the favoured methodology in relation to their day-to-day teaching.

CHILDREN WITH DIFFERENCES OR DIFFERENT CHILDREN?

One does not need to spend long in a special school to come across the 'what about Craig' syndrome. Craig usually has a female counterpart, whom we will call Debbie. Both will have failed to thrive in mainstream school but within weeks of being in a special school will have blossomed. Their low self-esteem will have been turned around. The success of their transfer to special school is quoted as the final denunciation of the principle of inclusion.

Their primary school case histories will be familiar to anyone in special education. The first concerns sprang from a feeling that they were somehow different from the other children in the class. Teachers felt unable to provide what they thought Craig and Debbie needed and thought that they would be better catered for in a special school, where there would be teachers who had the specialist knowledge to help them. Parents were won round, the procedures were gone through and the expectations that special school would be beneficial were realized.

After their transfer, their former teachers might have been in touch with the special school once or twice to see how they were getting on. They might have met a teacher from the special school and asked about them. The teacher may have said 'very well, in fact we are thinking of including them in our inclusion project'. At that point the primary school teacher would have had misgivings. Surely now the child was happy it would not make sense to put them back where they had experienced failure?

Parents, now relieved that their child was much happier at school, would have similar reservations. Thomas *et al.* (1998) describe one hurdle to inclusion as 'fear of the unknown'. For many children with learning or emotional difficulties, their parents and their teachers, it is more a fear of the known.

Feiler and Gibson (1999) reflect the view of many people working in special education that inclusion is being promoted on an ideological basis rather than as a result of strong empirical research findings. They point to a shortage of evidence in support of inclusion that, in their opinion, makes it easy for teachers to 'dismiss exhortations for inclusion' by raising issues about the detrimental effects on the children themselves and the disruption their presence will cause to the education of others.

There is no evidence that the education systems from which methodologies are being imported are any nearer to resolving these issues than are the countries where they are being adopted.

IMPORTED TEACHING APPROACHES

This leads us to ask 'are teaching methods imported from another system appropriate for all children in the host system?' Can the assertion that in a particular education system there is evidence that 'all children, including those with special needs, benefit from whole-class teaching' be substantiated? Before being able to answer that we must know whether the system actually segregates those who need regular individual support into separate classes or schools or, indeed, excludes them from the education system altogether.

Attempts to resolve this, can from experience, lead one into a circular debate which goes something like this:

- Are the teaching methods that are being promoted used with the children we feel would not cope with those approaches?

or

- Are the children we are thinking of taught through individualized approaches that would bear more relation to strategies being followed in our special schools, who are being exhorted to adopt the whole-class methods?
- Is the current belief in the effectiveness of Hungarian approaches based on evidence of its effectiveness with the whole-school population, or the general school population less those with special educational needs?

In other words we need to know if and where they draw a line between *mainstream* and *different*. We also need to ask whether they teach all children effectively, as Graham and colleagues (1999) suggest they do, without recognizing *differentiated learning* as a common feature of every class. Or could it be that because of the superiority of their approach children do not have learning difficulties? The distinct impression is that difference is reduced by setting according to ability, which leads to the conclusion that there are sets with low-attaining children. It does not help that, because the real agenda is raising standards rather than inclusion, the models of good practice being publicized are of teachers working with children of at least average attainment and often higher.

Such issues can be used to call into question any international comparisons of the effectiveness of educational approaches. The difficulty of being sure that one is comparing like with like should make us pause before basing innovation on what is happening elsewhere. It is perhaps more fruitful to look at how some schools seem to achieve more than others with children who exhibit a similar range of learning characteristics. Closer collaboration between schools, both locally and internationally, will illuminate the features of effective practice and lead to improved practice.

SCHOOLS BECOMING INCLUSIVE

Mathematics, a major element of the curriculum in all countries, is an area ripe for the development of inclusive practices. The examples are as yet scattered and perhaps at too tender a stage of development for the participants to feel comfortable about them being held up as models of good practice. Like true professionals they know that there is still a lot of work to be done before they can feel that every child is fully included in the mathematics teaching in the school.

Despite what has been said above, we should not close our eyes to the possibility that the benefits of interactive whole-class approaches may extend to the least able in a mixed-ability class and there are examples of this being so. It is one of the signs of movement from an exclusive to an inclusive view. Some opportunities have not yet been fully exploited, but in fairness it has to be said that there is a willingness to include all children within the ambit of many developmental projects.

PROCESS OF INCLUSION

On a national scale, curriculum initiatives such as the Numeracy Strategy are accompanied by favourable funding and support. It is at that moment that the inclusive element has to be introduced because that is when teachers are most receptive. Government exhortations about inclusion will not bear fruit if class teachers feel an unresolved tension between the demands for higher achievement and a naive assertion that the methods being promoted will result in greater inclusion.

As Straker (1997) has pointed out, the methods used in some school systems often result in a narrower ability range within classes and children with special needs being 'withdrawn from mainstream classes rather than integrated'. The corollary is that the inclusion of children with special needs into mainstream classes often results in a wider ability range in UK schools (Harris and Henkhuzens, 1998). Techniques such as whole-class teaching, developed for use with a narrow ability range, will create additional challenges for teachers having to use them with classes that include children whose learning characteristics might respond better to an alternative approach.

Now that British schools are expected to adopt Hungarian teaching methods, have we really begun to understand the shortcomings of this wholesale adoption of another methodology? We should be asking whether there are parallels to Ainscow's concerns about mainstream schools adopting special school practices.

Lavelle (1992) describes how up to 5 per cent of pupils in a Hungarian primary school are held back each year because they have not achieved the required standard in their work, a practice that is unlikely to find general acceptance in education systems that in grouping children give priority to maintaining them all in their age group. He also reports that maths is often the least popular subject because children can look foolish in front of their classmates when they fail to answer a question correctly. The comments quoted from Hungarian teachers seem to suggest that the pupils' self-esteem is not the issue with them that it is in some countries.

This is another illustration of how a single-focus initiative, such as raising standards in mathematics, does not always sit easily with the reality of classroom experience.

DECISION-MAKING LEVELS

For policy to become practice it has to go through several levels of action and the process has to be seen within the context of each level. At the political and administrative level there may be few participants who have recent experience of managing a school, let alone teaching in a classroom. The reverse is also true and it is important that channels of communication exist between those working in the different contexts.

Whilst the points that follow are related to the implementation in general terms of the principle of inclusion, they are relevant in that they relate to forces that will encourage or discourage the development of an inclusive approach to mathematics. Many of the discussions on inclusion take place at a policy level as was evident from the pro-gramme for a course entitled 'Inclusion: from Rhetoric to Reality' which had speakers from local authorities, universities and a government department. A line-up with that composition may address the political and resource conditions that can foster inclusion but it does not give a credible view from the two other levels that make or break inclusion.

There has to be commitment at a school level. Those with the final say on resource allocation — senior staff, local boards, managers or governors, depending on the structure of management within which the school works — need to make all their decisions within an inclusive context. We have pointed to the danger of mixed messages arising from tensions between raising standards overall and giving a higher resource loading to some children on the basis of need. Those tensions intensify the nearer one gets to the classroom and it is there that the process of inclusion either flourishes or withers.

'Fine words don't butter parsnips' and policy statements do not have much impact on the thousand of interpersonal interactions that occur each day in a classroom. We have tried to establish some indicators that would describe the form and texture of a classroom where inclusive mathematics was taking place. We have tried to disentangle definitions and opinions on what inclusion means and what it looks like. We have recognized that it is a process of renewal and development, not a fixed state. We do not pretend that it is fully achievable today but we should remember that today's impossibility often becomes tomorrow's reality.

CONCERNS OF TEACHERS

There is a tendency with the introduction of a new initiative for an overemphasis on 'what is to be taught' with the result that it is not seen in the wider context. Class teachers will, perhaps understandably, want to use their valuable time finding out what they are supposed to teach but those responsible for their training should be aware of the bigger picture. Some teachers are feeling under pressure to teach what is prescribed without understanding why. The Numeracy Strategy takes this a step further by dictating how mathematics should be taught. There is also direction on when and where particular topics should be taught. A profession that is not encouraged to question 'why' will be increasingly at the mercy of outside lobbies.

Teachers in special education have felt uncomfortable at having to justify their teaching in terms of relationship to key objectives, preferring, as they see it, to meet their children's needs by focusing on specific learning targets as stated in individual education plans (IEPs). There is, however, a recognition amongst teachers in the special schools that are involved in the Numeracy Strategy, that this should not preclude the children from participation in the richness of a well-taught mathematics lesson and they are seeing their pupils exceed their expectations when exposed to mathematics lessons in a mainstream school.

CURRICULUM CONVERGENCE OR DIVERGENCE?

For those kind of activities to be possible there must be a commonality to the curriculum that creates a shared vocabulary within which inclusive activities can be planned. The merit of the UK National Curriculum was in giving all teachers a readily understood means of describing their work and the capabilities of their children. It had its weaknesses in that special educational needs were not addressed at an earlier stage in its development but that has gradually been overcome and there are now the means for describing all children's learning experiences within a common framework.

Curriculum inclusion must begin with teachers; it does not stand alone. It depends upon social and attitudinal inclusion. It must be promoted at the policy stage and applied consistently through the planning, delivery and evaluation stages. It can only be achieved by taking every opportunity to bring convergence of the mainstream and special curriculum. There is a tendency to speak convergence but to practise divergence and to revert to comfort zones. An example of that phenomenon is when, on curriculum-focused courses, the mainstream and special school teachers return to their prospective camps for detailed discussion of 'what' and 'how'. This is understandable, but it perpetuates the divide between the mainstream and the special and reinforces the idea of specialism.

It is true that there are specialisms in teaching methodology, although, as explored in Chapter 4, it is debatable whether what is often regarded as a specialist pedagogy is in fact a version of normal teaching approaches. Most of the examples of classroom work given earlier are recognizable to teachers in both mainstream and special education, though the latter will point to modifications that they have made to make it accessible to their children.

We cannot define with any certainty the point at which this enhanced version of those generally recognizable approaches becomes something completely different. This leads into the dilemma of whether differentiation is an absolute or a matter of degree. Again, the situation is not static, but a dynamic one that moves with the changing responses that schools make to individual needs. Class or subject teachers have not, generally, received the training in the specialist skills of teaching deaf or blind children, but when working with a specialist teacher in the class some of the techniques 'rub off'. Teachers begin to take account of the strategies used by the specialist and assimilate them into their teaching.

This is more overtly the case where resource-base teachers in a mainstream school provide professional development for their colleagues. It then opens the door for teachers not only to teach but also to plan their teaching with consideration for specialist methodologies. In turn their own teaching is enhanced and could be described as 'good teaching plus'. Once that is embedded in the school it becomes, perhaps, no more than the expected standard for teaching in that school. It would only be considered 'good teaching plus' by being compared with what happens in a school that has not embraced specialist methodology in the same way.

Specialized training is necessary to learn techniques that are different from those normally used in the classroom, such as signing and Braille, which are associated with teaching children with serious hearing or visual problems. Teachers of the deaf recognize that they are often working in two languages, the mother tongue and sign language, and that the nuances of spoken language that give life and meaning to classroom interactions can be missed by the children they are supporting. The specialist training that both need to become effective in their role could not, on the grounds of time and cost, be provided for every classroom teacher.

For physical disabilities, learning difficulties and emotional and behavioural difficulties there is no formal requirement for specialist training, although many teachers take advanced courses that focus on these aspects of special needs. It is hotly debated as to whether good teaching per se is sufficient or whether there is a distinct methodology that has to be employed if teaching is to be effective.

At the time when children with severe and profound learning difficulties became the responsibility of the UK education system, separate initial training courses were established to create a cadre of teachers equipped to teach in the new special schools. A methodology, developed to make teaching meaningful to children with those problems and educational goals, was introduced in those schools.

In recent years, separate training is no longer considered necessary for teachers of children with severe learning difficulties (SLD), which brings them into line with those teaching children with moderate learning difficulties (MLD). The argument that teachers in MLD schools do not need specialized training holds true by default, in that most teachers in those schools have come from mainstream education with no specialist training. However, they have all had to recognize the need to adapt their normal approaches. The nature of such schools is that the children exhibit a wide range of learning and behavioural characteristics and new members of staff assimilate strategies they see being used by experienced colleagues.

The danger in relying on that as the sole means of professional development is that those teachers will adjust their expectations to conform to the prevailing culture of the school and the school will lose the benefits that can be brought by a fresh view of the education they should be providing. A teacher whose approach and expectations set a challenge to the 'way we do things in this school' will experience frustration and self-doubt, and probably knowing looks and comments from longer-serving colleagues. Teachers going with an inclusive philosophy into special schools will experience this kind of opposition. Many head teachers felt that the discontinuation of that training left them with the task of retraining teachers to work in their schools and they did not have a pool of fresh talent to draw upon. This suggests that from their experience normal teacher training does not equip teachers to work in special schools.

What is perceived as a gap is filled, partially, by continuing professional development from a number of sources, including local education authorities, universities, colleges and independent training organizations. This provision reflects a demand but many of the providers are concerned whether 'special education' as a title for their activities fits current thinking on inclusion.

Thomas *et al.* (1998) suggests that there is no magic formula for teaching children who experience difficulties. The main requirement is for creativity and imagination to make the curriculum come alive for children. The history of mathematics teaching shows that this is desirable for all children, not just those who are designated SEN. Those qualities are found in good teachers in all types of school and it would be a natural development of their skills to create conditions in which all children could thrive.

TEACHING MATHEMATICS

The training of teachers is part of the UK Numeracy Strategy but Prais and Luxton (1998) express concerns on whether it is sufficient. They believe that a considerable amount of retraining needs to be done on the methodology of whole-class teaching and that there should be more investment in developing detailed teaching materials.

They also believe that the notion that whole-class teaching helps slower-developing pupils warrants further investigation. It certainly contradicts the narrowing of the mathematics curriculum for children with special educational needs that has accompanied the growth of separate special education provision. The question as to whether a large number of teachers have been misguided in concentrating on what they believed to be the 'essentials of mathematics' has not been conclusively resolved.

SERVANT, CITIZEN OR SOVEREIGN

The analogy of mathematics as servant, citizen and sovereign (Higginson, 1999) is a useful one. The first two are applicable to children with special needs, but teachers often ask whether it is unrealistic to think of those children enjoying mathematics for its own sake.

The kind of project described by Higginson (referred to in Chapter 5) should prompt us into asking if it might be our view of mathematics that restricts children, not the subject itself or our perception of their needs in adult life. Mathematics can include all children, even if the current state of mathematics education has not achieved inclusion. Creating, describing and comparing patterns, number or geometrical, can be a very creative activity. The displays on the wall in a nursery or reception class and the investigative early mathematical activities taking place exemplify a subject that is definitely alive.

WHO BENEFITS FROM INCLUSIVE MATHEMATICS?

Hart (1996) contends that all children will benefit from strategies that are similar to those described in the second part of this book. Feiler and Gibson (1999) pick up this point and ask 'who benefits from inclusion?' Earlier we noted their concern that there is very little research with which to respond to this question.

In the context of inclusive mathematics we face a similar dilemma. Having set out the stall for an inclusive view of mathematical education it is to be hoped that the evaluation of initiatives to raise mathematical standards will include research into the benefits for those children whom the school system identifies as SEN. There seems to be a consistent message that the evidence of effective practice does not support the practice of having a wide range of ability in a class, which would be the natural consequence of inclusion. This leads to the conclusion that the adoption of a whole-class teaching methodology has weaknesses as a route towards inclusive mathematics if we stand firmly on the principles of inclusion.

PRINCIPLE OR PRAGMATISM?

The pragmatic response is that the ideal will be a stumbling block to progress and we have to work within the reality of schools today, with all the internal and external pressures that they have to face. If we take the principles of inclusive mathematics as school effectiveness goals and develop the means of achieving them within the expanding knowledge base of effective practice, then we may be setting ourselves a more manageable task. It would seem pointless to swim against the tide of what is generally considered to be the best way of raising achievement.

A more productive route would be to follow those principles through and to ask on a regular basis: 'that sounds fine for most of the class but how can we make sure that x and y benefit?' The SENCO might see this as part of their role, but any member of staff should feel free to raise the issue until it has become an established feature of the school's self-review process.

This will not completely answer the question set by Feiler and Gibson; that requires setting another challenging question: 'does the school's endeavour to make the curriculum fully inclusive have a beneficial or detrimental effect on overall standards of achievement?' If 'overall' is defined as 80 per cent of the children in the education system we will arrive at one set of answers. The true test of inclusive principles will be the findings that give equal value to the achievement of 100 per cent of the children in any age group in any country.

TALKING POINTS

Describe to a colleague the main points in this book.
What can you do to develop an inclusive approach to mathematics in your school?
What do you already do that accords with the principles set out in this book?
What changes could you make immediately?
What medium- and long-term innovations would encourage the inclusive process?

References

Ahmed, A. (1989) Better expectations, better achievement. In P. Widlake (ed.) *Special Children Handbook: Meeting Special Needs Within the Mainstream School*. Birmingham: Questions Publishing.

Ahmed, A. (1996) Better expectations, better achievement. In P. Widlake (ed.) *Good Practice Guide to Special Educational Needs*. Birmingham: Questions Publishing.

Ainscow, M. (1997) Towards inclusive schooling. *British Journal of Special Education* **24** (1), 3–6.

Ainscow, M., Farrell, P., Tweddle, D. and Malki, G. (1999) *Effective Practice in Inclusion and in Special and Mainstream Schools Working Together*. Research Report RR91. London: DfEE Publications.

Anderson, J. (1999) Being mathematically educated in the 21st century: what should it mean? In C. Hoyles, C. Morgan and G. Woodhouse (eds) *Rethinking the Mathematics Curriculum*. London: Falmer Press.

Aplin, R. (1998) *Assisting Numeracy: A Handbook for Classroom Assistants*. London: BEAM Education.

Arnold, R. (1995) *The Improvement of Schools Through Partnership: School, LEA, and University*. Slough: NFER.

Ashdown, R. and Devereux, K. (1990) Teaching mathematics to pupils with severe learning difficulties. In D. Baker and K. Bovair (eds) *Making the Special Schools Ordinary?* Vol. 2. London: Falmer Press.

Ashdown, R., Carpenter, B. and Bovair, K. (1991) *The Curriculum Challenge*. London: Falmer Press.

Aubrey, C. (1993) The primacy of pedagogy. *Special Children* (November/December 1993), 14–16.

Aubrey, C. (1998) Mathematics and the SENCO. *Special Children* **108** (February 1998), 1–7 (supplement)

Aubrey, C. (1999) Maths for the millennium. *Special Children* **122** (September 1999), Numeracy and special needs supplement, 2–8.

Ausubel, D. (1968) *Educational Psychology – A Cognitive View*. New York: Holt, Rinehart & Winston.

Bach, R. (1972) *Jonathan Livingston Seagull*. Great Britain: Turnstone Books.

Basic Skills Agency (1998) *Family Numeracy Adds Up: Lessons from the Family Numeracy Pilot Programme*. London: Basic Skills Agency.

Beard, R. (1969) *An Outline of Piaget's Developmental Psychology*. London: Routledge and Kegan Paul.

Bell, D. (1992) *Bright Ideas: Maths Projects*. Leamington Spa: Scholastic Publications.

Beveridge, S. (1998) Foreword. In T. Tilstone, L. Florian and R. Rose (eds) *Promoting Inclusive Practice*. London: David Fulton.

Bovair, K. and Robbins, B. (1996) Modern foreign languages. In B. Carpenter, R. Ashdown and K. Bovair (eds) *Enabling Access*. London: David Fulton.

Bower, T. G. R. (1977) *The Perceptual World of the Child*. Cambridge, Mass: Harvard University Press.

Boyd, B. and O'Neill, M. (1999) Raising achievement for all: North Lanarkshire's strategy for breaking the links between disadvantage and underachievement. *Support for Learning* **14** (2) (May 1999), 51–7.

Brighouse, T. and Woods, D. (1999) *How to Improve Your School*. London: Routledge.

Brown, M. (1999) One mathematics for all? In C. Hoyles, C. Morgan and G. Woodhouse (eds) (1999) *Rethinking the Mathematics Curriculum*. London: Falmer Press.

Brown, T. (1998) *Coordinating Mathematics Across the Primary School*. London: Falmer Press.

Burghes, D. (1996) Why we lag behind in maths. *The Times Educational Supplement*, 15 March 1996.

Burkhardt, H. (1999) Why do they do better? From a review of mathematical books, published in the *The Times Educational Supplement*, 12 March 1999.

Bynner, J. and Parsons, S. (1997) *Does Numeracy Matter?* London: Basic Skills Agency.

Chinn, S. and Ashcroft, R. (1996) Teaching mathematics to dyslexics. In P. Widlake (ed.) *Good Practice Guide to Special Educational Needs*. Birmingham: Questions Publishing.

Clausen-May, T. (1999) The hidden Einsteins. *Special Children* **117** (February 1999), 14–16.

Cockburn, A. (1999) *Teaching Mathematics with Insight*. London: Falmer Press.

Creese, A., Daniels, H. and Norwich, B. (1997) *Teacher Support Teams in Primary and Secondary Schools*. London: David Fulton.

CSIE (1996) *Developing an Inclusive Policy for Your School: A CSIE Guide*. Centre for Studies on Inclusive Education, 1 Redland Close, Elm Lane, Redland, Bristol, BS6 6UE.

Daniels, H. and Anghileri, J. (1995) *Secondary Mathematics and Special Educational Needs*. London: Cassell.

Denvir, B., Stolz, C. and Brown, M. (1982) *Low Attainers in Mathematics*. Schools Council Working Paper 72. London: Methuen Educational.

DES (1978) *Special Educational Needs: Report of the Committee of Enquiry into the Education of Handicapped Children and Young people* (The Warnock Report). London: HMSO.

DES (1982) *Mathematics Counts* (The Cockroft Report). London: HMSO.

DES (1988) *The Education Reform Act 1988*. London: HMSO.

DES (1989) *Non-statutory Guidance to the National Curriculum in Mathematics*. London: HMSO.

Dew-Hughes, D., Brayton, H. and Blandford, S. (1998) A survey of training and professional development for learning support assistants. *Support for Learning* **13** (4) (November 1998), 179–83.

DfE (1995) *Mathematics in the National Curriculum*. London: HMSO.

DfEE (1997) *Excellence for All Pupils*. London: HMSO.

DfEE (1999) *The National Numeracy Strategy: Framework for Teaching Mathematics*. London: DfEE Publications.

Donaldson, M. (1978) *Children's Minds*. Glasgow: Fontana/Collins.

EADSNE (1997) *Participation of Pupils and Students with Special Educational*

Needs in the Socrates Programme. Middelfart: European Agency for Development in Special Needs Education.

EADSNE (1999) *Teacher Support: Organisation of Support for Teachers Working with Special Needs in Mainstream Education.* Middelfart: European Agency for Development in Special Needs Education. Web site: *http://www. european-agency.org*

Evans, P. (1997) Structuring the curriculum for pupils with learning difficulties In S. J. Pijl, C. W. Meijer and S. Hegarty (eds), *Inclusive Education: A Global Agenda.* London: Routledge.

Feiler, A. and Gibson, H. (1999) Threats to the inclusive movement. *British Journal of Special Education* **26** (3) (September 1999), 147–52.

Fish, J. (1984) The future of the special school. In T. Bowers (ed.) *Management and the Special School.* London: Croom Helm.

Florian, L. (1998) Inclusive practice: what, why and how? In T. Tilstone, L. Florian and R. Rose (eds) *Promoting Inclusive Practice.* London: David Fulton.

Fraser, B. (1992) Hearing impairments. In R. Gulliford and G. Upton (eds) *Special Educational Needs.* London: Routledge.

Fullan, M. (1996) *Change Forces: Probing the Depths of Educational Reform.* London: Falmer Press.

Gardner, H. (1993) *Multiple Intelligences: The Theory in Practice.* New York: Basic Books.

Goodwins, S. (1999) Putting the pieces in place. *Special!* (Summer 1999), 8–11.

Graham, T., Rowlands, S., Jennings, S. and English, J. (1999) Towards whole-class interactive teaching. *Teaching Mathematics and its Applications* **18** (2), 50–60.

Griffiths, H. B. (1999) Fudge and fiddlesticks. In C. Hoyles, C. Morgan and G. Woodhouse (eds) *Rethinking the Mathematics Curriculum.* London: Falmer Press.

Gulliford, R. and Upton, G. (eds) (1992) *Special Educational Needs.* London: Routledge.

Halpin, D. and Lewis, A. (1996) The impact of the National Curriculum on twelve special schools in England. *European Journal of Special Needs Education* **11** (1), 95–105.

Harland, J. (1987) The TVEI experience: issues of control, response and the professional role of teachers. In D. Gleeson (ed.) *TVEI and Secondary Education: A Critical Appraisal.* Milton Keynes: Open University Press.

Harlen, W. and Malcolm, H. (1997) Assessment and testing in Scottish primary schools. *Curriculum Journal* **7** (2), 247–57.

Harris, S. and Henkhuzens, Z. (1998) *Mathematics in Primary Schools.* Slough: NFER.

Hart, S. (1996) *Beyond Special Needs.* London: Paul Chapman.

Hatano, G. (1997) Learning arithmetic with an abacus, In T. Nunes and P. Bryant (eds) *Learning and Teaching Mathematics: An International Perspective.* Hove: Psychology Press.

Hatch, G. (1999) Maximizing energy in the learning of mathematics. In C. Hoyles, C. Morgan and G. Woodhouse (eds) *Rethinking the Mathematics Curriculum.* London: Falmer Press.

Higginson, W. (1999) Glimpses of the past, images of the future: moving from twentieth to twenty-first century mathematics education. In C. Hoyles, C. Morgan and G. Woodhouse (eds) *Rethinking the Mathematics Curriculum*. London: Falmer Press.

Holt, J. (1969) *How Children Fail*. London: Pelican.

Hoyles, C., Morgan, C. and Woodhouse, G. (eds) (1999) *Rethinking the Mathematics Curriculum*. London: Falmer Press.

Jacobson, K. (1999) Categorical denial. *Special Children* **121** (July 1999), 14–16.

Jerwood, L. (1999) Using special needs assistants effectively. *British Journal of Special Education* **26** (3) (September 1999), 127–9.

Joffe, L. and Foxman, D. (1989) *Assessment of Performance Unit: Communicating Mathematical Ideas*. London: HMSO.

Jowett, S., Hegarty, S. and Moses, D. (1988) *Joining Forces: a Study of Links Between Special and Ordinary Schools*. Windsor: NFER-Nelson.

Knight, B. (1989) *Managing School Time*. Harlow: Longman.

Knight, B. A. (1999) Towards inclusion of students with special educational needs in the regular classroom. *Support for Learning* **14** (1) (February 1999), 3–7.

Lacey, P. and Ranson, S. (1994) Partnership for learning. In C. Gains (ed.) *Collaborating to Meet Special Educational Needs*. Stafford: NASEN.

Lavelle, A. (1992) Hungary for learning. *Junior Education*, October.

Lewis, A. (1991) *Primary Special Needs and the National Curriculum*. London: Routledge.

Lorenz, S. (1999) Thinking in figures. *Special!* (Spring 1999).

Mailhos, M-F., Lavelle, A. and Kruppa, E. (1996) *PETIT, Primary European Teachers in Training* (Report of TEMPUS project no. JEN 2158) Brussels: European Training Foundation of the European Union. ISBN 963 856690 6.

Manchester College of Education (1971) *Notes on Guidelines in School Mathematics*. St Albans: Hart-Davis Educational.

Marvin, C. (1998) Individual and whole class teaching. In T. Tilstone, L. Florian and R. Rose (eds) *Promoting Inclusive Practice*. London: David Fulton.

Mason, H. L. (1995) *Spotlight on Special Educational Needs: Visual Impairment*. Tamworth: NASEN Publications.

Matthews, G. (1990) *Early Mathematical Experiences* (3rd edn.) Harlow: Longman.

Meijer, C. (ed.) (1998) *Integration in Europe: Provision for Pupils with Special Educational Needs, Trends in 14 European Countries*. Middelfart: European Agency for Development in Special Needs Education.

Merttens, R (1991) New initiatives in primary maths. In M. Sullivan (ed.) *Supporting Change and Development in the Primary School*. Harlow: Longman.

Merttens, R. (1997) Active ingredients. *The Times Educational Supplement, Mathematics Extra*, 21 March 1997.

Millett, A., Brown, M. and Askew, M. (1995) Research focus on mathematics. *Child Education* **72** (8) (supplement)

Mosley, J (1993) *Turn Round your School*. Wisbech: LDA.

Muijs, D. (1999) *Evidence Base for a Numeracy Strategy*. Presentation at University of Birmingham, 7 July 1999. Contact: D. Muijs, Department of Education, University of Newcastle upon Tyne.

NCC (1992) *Curriculum Guidance 9: The National Curriculum and Pupils with Severe Learning Difficulties*. York: NCC.

Newton, M. (1999) Games Count. *Special Children* **116** (January 1999), Standards Supplement, 2–12.

NPC (1994) *The Open Door*. Oxford: National Primary Centre.

Ofsted (1997) *The Teaching of Number in Three Inner-urban LEAs*. London: Office for Standards in Education.

Ofsted (1998) *The National Numeracy Project: An HMI Evaluation*. London: Office for Standards in Education. Internet: *www.ofsted.gov.uk*

O'Toole, B. and O'Toole, P. (1989) How accessible is Level 1 Maths? *British Journal of Special Education* **16** (3), 115–18.

Parrilla, A. (1999) Educational innovations as a school answer to diversity. *International Journal of Inclusive Education* **3** (10), 93–110.

Piaget, J. (1952) *The Child's Conception of Number*. London: Routledge and Kegan Paul.

Prais, S. J. and Luxton, R. (1998) Are the proposed reforms of numeracy teaching sufficient for success? *Teaching Mathematics and its Applications* **17** (4), 145–51.

Pyke, N. (1996) British maths fails to add up. *The Times Educational Supplement*, 15 March 1996.

Read, G. (1998) Promoting inclusion through learning styles. In T. Tilstone, L. Florian and R. Rose (eds) *Promoting Inclusive Practice*. London: David Fulton.

Reynolds, M. C. (1989) Students with special needs. In M. C. Reynolds (ed.) *The Knowledge Base of the Beginning Teacher*. Oxford: Pergamon.

Rhydderch-Evans, Z. (1989) In my view. *Child Education* (April 1989).

Robbins, B. (1978) *Step by Small Step – A Structured Approach to Pre-number Learning*. Wisbech: LDA.

Robbins, B. (1981) Mathematics for slow-learners: curriculum development through materials evaluation. Unpublished MEd dissertation. University of Birmingham.

Robbins, B. (1989) There's a place for us. *Junior Education* (October 1989).

Robbins, B. (1991a) Mathematics for all. In B. Carpenter, R. Ashdown and K. Bovair (eds) *The Curriculum Challenge*. London: David Fulton.

Robbins, B. (1991b) *Erste Schritte Mathe*. Mulheim: Verlag an der Ruhr.

Robbins, B. (1993) Sans frontières. *Special Children* (April 1993).

Robbins, B. (1995) Links across Europe. *Special!* **4** (1) (Spring 1995).

Robbins, B. (1996) *Mathsteps* (3rd edn.). Wisbech: LDA.

Rose, R. (1998) Including pupils – developing a partnership in learning. In T. Tilstone, L. Florian and R. Rose (eds) *Promoting Inclusive Practice*. London: David Fulton.

RSA (1997) *Key Skills Units*. RSA Examinations Board, Westwood Way, Coventry CV4 8HS.

SCAA (1994) *The National Curriculum and its Assessment; Final Report*. London: SCAA.

Sebba, J. and Ainscow, M. (1996) International developments in inclusive schooling: mapping the issues. *Cambridge Journal of Education* **26** (1), 5–17.

Sharpe, R. (1993) All done with beads. *Special Children* **3** (4), 31–2.

Skemp, R. (1971) *Psychology of Learning Mathematics*. London: Penguin.

164   *References*

Smith, B. (ed.) (1990) *Interactive Approaches to Teaching the Core Subjects.* Bristol: Lame Duck Publishing.

Smith, G. J. (1996) The consultant from Oz. In *Teaching Exceptional Children* (Summer 1996), 10–13.

Straker, A. (1997) Calculated pragmatism. *The Times Educational Supplement,* **4215** (11 April), 20.

Strang, J. D. and Rourke, B. P. (1985) Arithmetic disability sub-types: the neuro-psychological significance of specific arithmetic impairment in children. In B. P. Rourke (ed.) *Neuro-psychology of Learning Disabilities: Essentials of Sub-type Analysis.* New York: Guilford Press.

Swann, W. (1998) Learning difficulties or curricular reform: integration or differentiation?. In G. Thomas and A. Feiler (eds) *Planning for Special Needs: A Whole-School Approach.* Oxford: Basil Blackwell.

Tansley, A. E. and Gulliford, R. (1960) *The Education of Slow Learning Children.* London: Routledge.

Thomas, G., Walker, W. and Webb, J. (1998) *The Making of the Inclusive School.* London: Routledge.

UNESCO (1994) *The Salamanca Statement and Framework for Action on Special Needs Education.* Paris: UNESCO.

Walsh, A. (ed.) (1988) *Help your Child with Maths.* London: BBC Books.

Williams, A. (1992) Mathematics in transition. In K. Bovair, B. Carpenter and G. Upton (eds) *Special Curricula Needs.* London: David Fulton.

Wiltshire, A. (1998) A wider role for special schools? In T. Tilstone, L. Florian and R. Rose (eds) *Promoting Inclusive Practice.* London: David Fulton.

Index